108 課綱適用

英語 Make Me High 系列

學測英文
混合題 實戰演練

附解析本

溫宥基

學歷／
國立政治大學教育系博士
英國艾希特大學應用語言學所碩士
國立成功大學外國語文學系學士

經歷／
臺北市立和平高級中學校長
國立政治大學附屬高級中學英語教師

三民書局

序

英語 Make Me High 系列的理想在於超越，在於創新。

這是時代的精神，也是我們出版的動力；

這是教育的目的，也是我們進步的執著。

針對英語的全球化與未來的升學趨勢，

我們設計了一系列適合普高、技高學生的英語學習書籍。

面對英語，不會徬徨不再迷惘，學習的心徹底沸騰，

心情好 High ！

實戰模擬，掌握先機知己知彼，百戰不殆決勝未來，

分數更 High ！

選擇優質的英語學習書籍，才能激發學習的強烈動機；

興趣盎然便不會畏懼艱難，自信心要自己大聲說出來。

本書如良師指引循循善誘，如益友相互鼓勵攜手成長。

展書輕閱，你將發現……

學習英語原來也可以這麼 High ！

給讀者的話

　　《學測英文混合題實戰演練》是一本適合老師上課用，更適合學生自學使用的混合題題本。

　　為因應素養學習，使命題更多元活潑，避免單一選擇題的負面效果，大考中心自 111 學年度起，在英文科學測試題中設計混合題型，引導學生循序漸進的思考能力，並發展多層次評量。

　　混合題是以題組的方式呈現，閱讀完一篇文章之後，會有 3－4 小題。文章的內容可能是各類型的文本，也可能會是社群網路貼文與留言等非連續性文本，有可能加入表格或圖表，考驗學生是否能運用「略讀、掃讀、歸納與統整、指涉及推論、辨識作者的寫作態度、熟練語意及語法知識」等閱讀理解能力。

　　本書依據大考中心混合題型設計及測驗重點，精選不同類型的文本，主題也涉略許多重要議題。每篇文本都搭配擬真的混合題組，題型有多選題、簡答題、句子填充題、填表題、填號題、圖片配合題、單詞填空題以及四選一的選擇題。這本書可以協助學生為考試做準備，也可以增進閱讀理解能力。

本書在第一、第二單元提供混合題的閱讀策略及解題技巧，可幫助學生建立整體的作答思維。之後的單元則提供針對文章主題的暖身問題，有利老師引導學生討論。本書亦收錄文章的重要字彙片語和例句，學生能一併複習大考字彙。夾冊則提供文章中譯及搭配閱讀策略和解題技巧的詳解，讓學生內化混合題的考試邏輯。

　　《學測英文混合題實戰演練》完全仿照大考中心混合題設計及測驗重點書寫完成，架構精簡，但內容紮實精純，老師授課、學生自學練習皆無負擔。我相信，只要按照本書指引，掌握閱讀策略，勤加練習，一定能幫助同學在混合題取得高分。

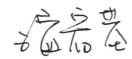

使用說明

本書分為兩部分：

第 1 至 2 單元為 **策略篇**，第 3 至 14 單元為 **實戰篇**。

透過閱讀策略，培養實戰技巧。

Step 1.

閱讀 Unit 1~2「策略篇」，熟悉混合題的命題核心。

介紹閱讀策略、大考常見題型
和答題技巧

搭配對應的練習題
立即應用

Step 2.

練習 Unit 3~14「實戰篇」，訓練混合題解題能力。

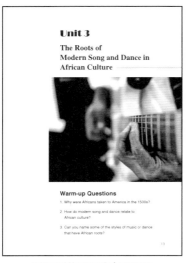

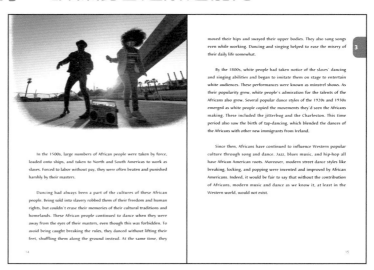

開頭搭配暖身問題
引導思考

閱讀主題文本

搭配仿學測混合題組
精熟學測出題模式

收錄文章重要字彙和片語，並提供例句
一併強化大考字彙力

Step 3.

搭配解析夾冊，強化應試邏輯、內化作答要點。

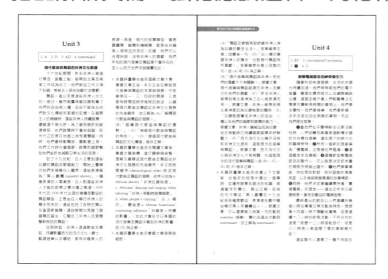

解析結合「策略篇」閱讀技巧
並附文章中譯

使用錯題筆記
釐清誤答原因
歸納專屬學習筆記

Table of Contents

Unit 1 策略篇 (上)

　　混合題的文本可能是一篇約 350 字的長篇閱讀文章，也可能是一篇廣告或網路貼文。不論是哪一類閱讀文本，題目測試重點在評量學生能否掌握兩個層次的試題：**整體理解試題 (global items) 及局部理解試題 (local items)**。整體理解試題在測試學生能否「掌握文章整體概念、主旨、寫作目的，並能系統化整合文本資訊」；局部理解試題則在測試學生能否「掌握語意及語法的知識、尋找特定資訊，並加以分析推論資訊」。

　　不論是哪一類的閱讀理解試題，學生都可以透過第一、二單元介紹的閱讀技巧，搭配相對應的試題練習，熟悉閱讀理解及考試作答技巧。本單元介紹其中三種常見的閱讀技巧：

一、略讀 (skimming)：

　　找出文章的主題句 (topic sentence) 或主題論述 (thesis statement)。

　　以單一段落來說，主題句通常落在該段的第一句；以長篇閱讀文本來說，主題論述通常落在第一段的最後一句。透過略讀各段落的第一句或是文章第一段的最後一句，可以快速有效掌握文章的整體概略大意或主旨。

二、辨識作者的寫作態度 (identifying the author`s attitude)：

　　利用關鍵字詞，推敲作者態度。

　　除陳述事實 (facts) 之外，閱讀時可留意作者是否表達自己的意見 (opinions)。特別注意作者在表達意見時的用字遣詞及語氣，利用上下文線索，推敲作者陳述主題的口吻及角度 (懷疑、樂觀、客觀或是感到灰心)，有時可以在文章的最後一段找到線索，再次確認作者語氣及態度。

三、歸納與統整 (summarizing and integrating)：

　　整合文本資訊，以表格方式進行統整。

　　運用理解與整合能力，將文本裡獨自分別的零碎資訊，進行有效連結，統整片斷資訊成為系統性的表格，深化全文理解能力。

現有混合題型大致可分七大類：**四選一選擇題、填號題、填表題、多選題、單詞填空題、句子填充題，以及簡答題**。而這七大類型會測試不同的閱讀理解技巧，從文本的訊息提取、廣泛理解，到統整解釋，都有可能是混合題型測試的重點。本書分兩單元介紹混合題型及閱讀技巧，搭配對應試題做說明，但也要提醒同學，不要死記題型及考點，而要熟練並活用閱讀技巧，才能戰勝混合題型。本單元介紹混合題三種出題形式：四選一選擇題、填號題、填表題。說明及示例如下：

一、四選一選擇題：

根據文章之文意及題目，從四個選項中，選出一個最適當的選項。選項可能是單詞、句子、文意脈絡的排列順序，或是圖示等。

【四選一選擇題示例】(取自 111 學測英文參考試卷第 47 題)

According to the passage, which of the following best describes the author's attitude towards the health benefits of superfoods?

(A) Doubtful.　　　(B) Optimistic.　　　(C) Objective.　　　(D) Frustrated.

【四選一選擇題示例說明】

本題評量學生能否**掌握文章大意並判斷作者的態度**，並從四個選項中選出一個選項，對應作者對超級食物的態度。

二、填號題：

將文章某一段落的所有句子標記號碼，學生依題目指示，回答號碼即可。

【填號題示例】(取自 111 學測英文參考試卷第 48 題)

The sentences in paragraph 3 are numbered ❶ to ❼. Which sentence best indicates the author's attitude toward chia seeds? Write down the **NUMBER** of the sentence on the answer sheet.

【填號題示例說明】

本題評量學生能否**判斷作者的態度，並加以舉證**，選出正確的句子編號，說明作者的態度。

三、填表題：

此類題型聚焦在多項重要事件、人名、概念等 (專有) 名詞或關鍵字，答案可能是單一字詞、字塊 (word chunk)，或文句片段。作答時要參考其他欄位的字詞，以相同的詞性填寫在對應的欄位中。

【填表題示例】(取自 111 學測英文參考試卷第 50 題)

Fill in the blanks with the information contained in the passage about kale and chia seeds.

	nutrient(s)	**benefit(s) of the nutrient(s)**
kale	iron and vitamins	(B) _____
chia seeds	(A) _____	protect against cardiovascular disease

【填表題示例說明】

本題評量學生能否**整合資訊**，辨認兩種超級食物的營養成分及其益處，並**以表格方式進行統整**。作答時可參考同一欄位的字詞，以相同的詞性填寫在對應的欄位中。空格 (A) 對應其上方的欄位，填入名詞；空格 (B) 對應其下方的欄位，填入以原形動詞為首的文句片段。

介紹完三種閱讀技巧及三類混合題型後，請閱讀接下來的文章，測試一下你的身手。

Robin Hood is a well-known fictional hero—a bold and daring character who took money from the rich to give to the poor. Today, the generous spirit of Robin Hood is kept alive in New York City by a charity organization bearing his name.

According to the Robin Hood website, nearly one million and eight hundred thousand New Yorkers live in poverty, even though the city enjoys a reputation among the world's wealthiest.

The Robin Hood Organization collects money from people who want to help the less-fortunate, and distributes it to deserving charities and community non-profit groups in the city. The organization carefully evaluates the charities and non-profits that apply to it for assistance, and determines which ones have the best chances of success before the money is turned over to them.

Around two hundred groups benefit thanks to the hardworking directors and staff at Robin Hood. The city's homeless can escape the cold, wet, hard life on the streets, at least temporarily, by sleeping in shelters that the organization helps to pay for. The poor can receive nourishment at soup kitchens and food banks the organization runs. The unemployed, struggling single parents, the disabled, and new immigrants escaping war in their own countries can find encouragement, skills training, and jobs through the agency of Robin Hood.

❶ Besides the financial support, Robin Hood helps groups dedicated to fighting poverty by giving them buildings, or space in buildings, to use at no cost. ❷ Freed from the burden of paying rents, these groups can devote more resources to serving clients. ❸ Robin Hood also helps groups to manage their day-to-day operations. ❹ Many organizations use this support since they may have the desire to help others, but lack practical experience that would enable them to do so effectively. ❺ If Robin Hood were alive today, he would be proud!

1. According to the passage, which of the following best describes the author's attitude toward the Robin Hood Organization?

(A) Ironic.　　　　(B) Concerned.　　　　(C) Admiring.　　　　(D) Humorous.

【參考答案】C

【解析說明】

本題評量學生能否掌握文章大意並判斷作者的態度。文章中作者明確舉出 Robin Hood Organization 為幫助弱勢所提供的協助；此外，作者在談論該組織的用字遣詞也多為正面肯定語氣 (如generous spirit、help the less-fortunate、carefully evaluates)，因此可判斷作者持讚賞的 (Admiring) 態度，故 (C) 為正解。(A) 挖苦的、(B) 擔憂的、(D) 幽默的。

2. The sentences in paragraph 5 are numbered ❶ to ❺. Which sentence best indicates the author's attitude toward the Robin Hood Organization? Write down the **NUMBER** of the sentence.

【參考答案】❺

【解析說明】

本題評量學生能否判斷作者的態度，並加以舉證。題目問第五段的哪一句話最能顯示作者對 Robin Hood Organization 的態度。第五段的前四句描述該組織如何給予協助，第五句 If Robin Hood were alive today, he would be proud!「如果羅賓漢今日還活著，他一定會感到驕傲！」，表示羅賓漢會對該組織感到驕傲，可驗證作者讚賞的態度。故正解為❺。

3. Fill in the blanks with the information contained in the passage about what the Robin Hood Organization does to help their clients.

clients	help and support(s)
· the homeless	· provide shelters for them to sleep in
· the poor	· (A) _____
· the unemployed · single parents · (B) _____ · new immigrants	· give encouragement, skills training, and jobs
· groups which fight poverty	· (C) _____ · help to manage their day-to-day operations

【參考答案】(A) give nourishment; (B) the disabled;

　　　　　　(C) give them buildings, or space in buildings, to use at no cost

【解析說明】

本題評量學生能否整合資訊，辨認 Robin Hood Organization 服務的對象及其相對應的協助項目，並以表格方式進行統整。

空格 (A) 和 (C) 須對應同一欄，填入以原形動詞為首的文句片段。空格 (A) 對應的服務對象為 the poor (窮人)，第四段第三句提到窮人獲得營養品 (nourishment)，因此該組織給予窮人營養品，故空格 (A) 正解為 give nourishment；空格 (C) 對應的服務對象為 groups which fight poverty (對抗貧窮的團體)，第五段第一句提到該組織給予這些團體建築物或建築物裡的空間作免費使用，故空格 (C) 正解為 give them buildings, or space in buildings, to use at no cost。

空格 (B) 須對應同一欄，填入名詞。空格 (B) 對應的服務項目為給予鼓勵、技能訓練和工作，第四段第四句提到失業者、艱困的單親父母、身障者和逃離家鄉戰亂的新移民可以找到鼓勵、技能訓練和工作，故空格 (B) 正解為 the disabled。

Unit 2　策略篇 (下)

　　「局部理解試題」是混合題型的重點測驗項目，測驗學生能否理解文意與掌握文章細節，運用語意及語法的知識作答，或尋找特定資訊，加以整合、分析。本單元再介紹另外常見的三種閱讀技巧：

一、掃讀 (scanning)：

　　尋找題目或選項中的「關鍵字」。

　　關鍵字可能是與文章主題有關的數據、時間、地點、專有名詞、原因、舉例等，考試時不妨在試題本上將這些關鍵字圈選出來，有助勾勒閱讀重點。

二、熟練語意及語法知識 (expanding vocabulary and grammar knowledge)：

　　字詞搭配 (collocations) 及語法結構是閱讀理解的基本要素。

　　面對多元的閱讀素材，學生除熟記單字及文法外，要能熟練單一字彙在不同文本及搭配字詞上所產生的不同字義；而辨識句法結構，刪減語句的干擾資訊，找出語意核心，更是掌握文章細節、理解文本的要素。

三、指涉 (reference) 及推論 (inference)：

　　連結資訊，理解上下文脈絡。

　　文章指涉的對象可能是某個特定的專有名詞 (如 Robin Hood)、明確的對象 (如 the village)、不特定的對象 (如 a young man) 或是代名詞 (如 it)。先清楚辨識作者指涉的對象為何，再藉由其他字詞提供的資訊，合理判斷作者想傳達的訊息。

 混合題型介紹

　　除長篇閱讀外，混合題型的文本可能是廣告、網路社群媒體貼文或是內含圖表的文本。除了第一單元介紹的四選一選擇題、填號題及填表題外，本單元介紹多選題、單詞填空題、句子填充題，以及簡答題，相關示例及說明如下：

一、多選題：

根據文意，從數個選項中選出多個適當的選項。選項可能是單詞、句子片段或完整句子。

【多選題示例】(取自 111 學測英文試卷第 49 題)

請從下列 (A) 到 (F) 中，選出對 Yusra Mardini 和 Popole Misenga 都正確的選項。(多選題)

(A) Being an Olympic medalist.

(B) Growing up in an orphanage.

(C) Joining the Olympic Games more than once.

(D) Leaving his/her hometown because of war.

(E) Showing talent in sports after going to a foreign country.

(F) Traveling through several countries before securing protection.

【多選題示例說明】

本題評量學生能否在閱讀文章後，**搜尋和整合**與 Yusra Mardini 和 Popole Misenga 有關的**特定資訊**，並從數個選項中選出多個選項。

二、單詞填空題：

此類題型需從文章中挑選單詞填入，並視語法需要，作動詞、名詞、形容詞或副詞的詞類變化；若填入動詞，需考量時態，填入原形動詞、第三人稱單數形、過去分詞或現在分詞；若填入名詞，則需考量單複數形態。

【單詞填空題示例】(取自 111 學測英文試卷第 47 題)

請根據選文內容，從兩則故事中各選出一個單詞 (word)，分別填入下列兩句的空格，並視語法需要作適當的字形變化，使句子語意完整、語法正確，且符合全文文意。(填空)

With her amazing courage and swimming skills, Yusra Mardini was not only able to save lives but also fulfill her dream of __(A)__ in the Olympic Games.

Judo helped Popole Misenga to be strong both physically and mentally, and gave him the courage to escape from the __(B)__ of his coaches.

【單詞填空題示例說明】

本題評量學生能否依據上下文脈絡，從指定的段落中選出一個單詞，並**運用語意及語法的知識**，做適當字形變化，寫出正解。

三、句子填充題：

　　此類題型評量學生能否掌握文意及語法結構 (如動詞結構的刪略法)，根據上下文脈絡將省略的字詞填入，答案常是文句片段。此類題型也會使用到「指涉及推論」的閱讀策略，評量學生能否連結資訊，理解上下文脈絡，擷取題目所指涉的特定字詞，了解文章指涉的對象並作答。

【句子填充題示例】(取自 111 學測英文參考試卷第 49 題)

What does the author mean by saying "... if you don't" in the last paragraph?

It means "... if you don't _____, no superfood will save you."

【句子填充題示例說明】

本題評量學生能否**掌握文意及語法結構**，理解 don't 之後省略了前述句子所提及的一般動詞片語：eat a balanced diet with plenty of fruit and vegetables and do regular exercise。

四、簡答題：

　　測驗內容多聚焦在概念、人名、事件等 (專有) 名詞或關鍵字 (句)，只會存在一個無庸置疑的答案。簡答題的答案可能是單一字詞、字塊 (word chunk) 或是完整句子。

【簡答題示例】(取自 111 學測英文試卷第 48 題)

Which word in Popole Misenga's story means "protection given by a country or embassy to refugees from another country"? (簡答，2 分)

【簡答題示例說明】

本題評量學生能否理解文意，**擷取題目所指涉的特定字詞或文句**，填入單一字詞、字塊 (word chunk) 或完整句子。

　　介紹完三種閱讀技巧及四類混合題型後，請閱讀接下來的文章，測試一下你的身手。

When it comes to purchasing groceries, consumers must choose what to put in their shopping carts, and what to leave out. One choice involves whether to purchase so-called junk food, which is cheap and tasty but low in nutrition, or healthier "whole foods" like unprocessed fruits, vegetables and meat. Leaving junk food aside, even if you go for whole foods, a second choice must be made: do you want to eat organic or genetically modified (GM) food? Here are some views and thoughts associated with both kinds.

Organic food is grown without using chemical fertilizers to promote plant growth or spraying other chemicals on crops to keep insects away. Natural methods are used to attain these goals instead. As a result, organic food is healthier, since many chemicals commercial farmers typically use are actually harmful to humans. On the other hand, because farmers don't rely on the convenience of chemicals, growing organic fruits and vegetables is more time-consuming and labor-intensive. This makes them more expensive compared to ones grown using regular commercial methods. Finally, organic produce is often smaller than GM fruits and vegetables, and tends to be less uniform in appearance. It may even show signs of being bit by insects.	GM crops tend to be bigger, with uniform size, shape, and color. In fact, the specific strains of plant species available in most supermarkets have been specifically bred in laboratories for these qualities. Benefits of growing GM crops include increased crop yields, diminished use of substances that kill pests, and increased profits. Thus, most large farms do so. The resulting economies of scale also make growing them cheaper. The cost saving gets passed on to consumers. The farming of GM crops has massively increased since the mid-1990s. Last but not least, GM crops are one way to make enough nutritious food available with limited land, water, and other resources as the population grows fast.

PS: Marketing food as organic or selling food with an organic label on the wrapping is regulated by the governmental food safety authority.

1. 請根據選文內容，從兩欄中各選出一個單詞 (word)，分別填入下列兩句的空格，並視語法需要作適當的字形變化，使句子語意完整、語法正確，且符合全文文意。(填空)

Organic agriculture may restrict the use of certain ___(A)___ substances and fertilizers in the farming process, and thus has higher production costs, higher labor costs, and higher selling prices.

Most GM crops have been developed to improve production through the introduction of resistance to ___(B)___ or plant diseases, which can allow for reductions in food prices.

【參考答案】(A) chemical; (B) pests

【解析說明】

本題評量學生能否依據上下文脈絡，從指定的段落中各選出一個單詞，並運用語意及語法的知識，作適當的字形變化，寫出正解。

左欄談論有機食品 (organic food) 的種植過程「不採用化學肥料也不噴灑化學物質」及「高生產成本」，搭配空格 (A) 的句子陳述「有機農業在耕種過程中可能會限制特定**化學**物質和肥料的使用，因此具有較高的生產成本、較高的勞力成本以及較高的銷售價格」，可以選出左欄的形容詞 chemical (化學的)，故空格 (A) 正解為 chemical。

右欄談論基改食品 (GM food) 的特質，包含生產成本較低、減少殺蟲劑的使用、對大量生產有所助益，搭配空格 (B) 的句子陳述「大多的基改作物由對**害蟲**或植物疾病抵抗性的引入做發展，以提升產量，這讓糧食價格得以減低」，可以選出右欄的名詞 pests (害蟲)，故空格 (B) 正解為 pests。

2. 請從下列 (A) 到 (F) 中，選出對 organic food 和 GM crops 都正確的選項。
(多選題)

(A) Organic produce and GM crops are both available in supermarkets.

(B) There are health concerns associated with both organic and GM foods.

(C) Organic crops are grown in nature, while GM crops are grown in laboratories.

(D) Compared to GM food, the organic one is more appealing in appearance.

(E) More people are willing to spend more money on organic products than GM ones.

(F) Organic food is more expensive compared to GM food due to the farming cost.

【參考答案】(A)，(F)

【解析說明】

本題評量學生能否做局部細節的吸收，理解有機食品和基改食品的概念，並進行綜合分析。(A)「有機食品和基改作物都可在超市中買得到。」；(F)「因為耕種成本的因素，有機食品較基改食品貴。」故 (A) 和 (F) 為正解。

(B)「有機食品與基改食品都有健康上的疑慮。」文章裡沒有討論基改食品的健康疑慮；(C)「有機作物種植於大自然中，而基改作物種植於實驗室中。」文章裡提到基改作物是在實驗室中育種 (breed)，而非種植於實驗室；(D)「與基改食品相較，有機食品在外觀上較吸引人。」文章指出基改食品外觀較有機食品吸引人；(E)「更多人願意花錢在有機食品上，而非基改食品。」文章只提到有機食品價格較昂貴，但沒有指出有更多人願意花錢購買它。故 (B)、(C)、(D) 和 (E) 皆非正解。

3. What does the author mean by saying "Thus, most large farms do so" in the right column?

It means "Thus, most large farms _____."

【參考答案】grow GM crops

【解析說明】

本題評量學生能否掌握文意及語法結構，根據上下文脈絡將省略的字詞填入。作答線索在前一句 Benefits of growing GM crops include increased crop yields, diminished use of substances that kill pests, and increased profits「種植基改作物的好處有增加農作物產量，減少殺蟲劑的使用，以及增加利潤」。因此，多數大型農場會這麼做，指的就是種植基改作物，故正解為 grow GM crops。

4. Which institution makes sure that customers can easily identify organic food from the label on the food wrapping? (簡答)

【參考答案】the governmental food safety authority

【解析說明】

本題評量學生能否理解文意，從文中擷取題目所指涉的特定字詞作為答案。作答線索在文章最後一句 Marketing food as organic or selling food with an organic label on the wrapping is regulated by the governmental food safety authority「銷售有機食品或在食品外包裝上貼有機標籤，是由政府的食品安全機關來規範」。這一句指涉的涵義為，政府的食品安全機關會把關，確保消費者可從食物包裝上的有機標籤，清楚辨識有機食品，故正解為 the governmental food safety authority。

Unit 3

The Roots of Modern Song and Dance in African Culture

Warm-up Questions

1. Why were Africans taken to America in the 1500s?

2. How do modern song and dance relate to African culture?

3. Can you name some of the styles of music or dance that have African roots?

In the 1500s, large numbers of African people were taken by force, loaded onto ships, and taken to North and South Americas to work as slaves. Forced to labor without pay, they were often beaten and punished harshly by their masters.

Dancing had always been a part of the cultures of these African people. Being sold into slavery robbed them of their freedom and human rights, but couldn't erase their memories of their cultural traditions and homelands. These African people continued to dance when they were away from the eyes of their masters, even though this was forbidden. To avoid being caught breaking the rules, they danced without lifting their feet, shuffling them along the ground instead. At the same time, they moved their hips and swayed their upper bodies. They also sang songs even while working. Dancing and singing helped to ease the misery of their daily life somewhat.

By the 1800s, white people had taken notice of the slaves' dancing and singing abilities and began to imitate them on stage to entertain white audiences. These performances were known as minstrel shows. As their popularity grew, white people's admiration for the talents of the Africans also grew. Several popular dance styles of the 1920s and 1930s emerged as white people copied the movements they'd seen the Africans making. These included the jitterbug and the Charleston. This time period also saw the birth of tap-dancing, which blended the dances of the Africans with other new immigrants from Ireland.

Since then, Africans have continued to influence Western popular culture through song and dance. Jazz, blues music, and hip-hop all have African American roots. Moreover, modern street dance styles like breaking, locking, and popping were invented and improved by African Americans. Indeed, it would be fair to say that without the contribution of Africans, modern music and dance as we know it, at least in the Western world, would not exist.

_____ 1. What is the main idea of this passage? (單選)

(A) To explain the development of modern music and dance.

(B) To advocate the advantages of modern music and dance.

(C) To examine the characteristics of modern music and dance.

(D) To promote the cultural value of modern music and dance.

_____ 2. In what order is the passage organized? (單選)

a. African Americans' continuing influence

b. African slavery

c. Africans' dancing and singing while laboring

d. white people's copying

(A) d → c → a → b   (B) c → d → b → a

(C) c → b → a → d   (D) b → c → d → a

_____ 3. 請從下列 (A) 到 (F) 中，選出對文章發展及細節敘述正確的選項。(多選題)

(A) Dancing and singing helped to reduce the hardships of Africans working as slaves.

(B) Modern music and dance have little to do with African people and their contribution.

(C) Many African people were taken to North and South Americas to put on shows for the whites.

(D) White people copied the Africans' dance movements, which also contributed to modern dance.

(E) Slavery robbed African people of their freedom, human rights, and their abilities to sing and dance.

(F) Western popular culture mixed with little African culture has contributed to modern music and dance.

4. 請根據選文內容，從第三段選出一個單詞 (word)，填入下列句子的空格，並視語法需要作適當的字形變化，使句子語意完整、語法正確，且符合文意。(填空)

The minstrel shows were extremely popular during the 1800s, in which the performers _____ white people with their imitations of the Africans.

重要字彙

1. **load** (*v.*) 裝載 ②
   - The mail carrier **loaded** all the packages into the delivery van and took off.
     郵差將所有的包裹裝進廂型貨車裡，然後把車開走。

2. **force** (*n.*) 暴力；(*v.*) 強迫 ②
   - Facing the armed suspect, the police had no choice but to use **force**.
     警察面對武裝嫌犯，只能別無選擇使用暴力。

   - It is against the law for employers to **force** their employees to work overtime.
     雇主強迫員工加班是違法的。

3. **labor** (*v.*) 勞動 ④
   - David has been **laboring** all day to try to get his assignment done.
     David 勞動了一整天，試著完成他的工作。

4. **harshly** (*adv.*) 惡劣地
   - Elena was treated **harshly** by her ex-partner, so she became afraid of entering a new relationship.
     Elena 受到前伴侶惡劣地對待，因此她變得害怕展開新關係。

   harsh (*adj.*) 惡劣的 ④
   - This kind of crop grows well even in a **harsh** environment.
     這種作物即便在惡劣的環境裡也長得很好。

5. **master** (*n.*) 主人 ②
   - In the old days, the lives of the servants are controlled by their **masters**.
     在過去，僕人的性命由他們的主人所掌控。

6. **slavery** (*n.*) 奴隸制度 ⑤
   - After the American Civil War, the United States banned **slavery** in the whole country.
     美國內戰之後，美國禁止了全國的奴隸制度。

7. **erase** (*v.*) 抹去 ③
   - The ancient town was **erased** from existence by a powerful earthquake.
     這座古城被一場強烈的地震從地表上抹去。

8. **forbidden** (*adj.*) 禁止的 ④
   - It is **forbidden** for students to wander around campus after 10 p.m.
     晚上十點後學生禁止在校園裡閒晃。

9. **avoid** (*v.*) 避免 ②

· Lisa **avoids** going to places crowded with too many people during flu season.
Lisa 避免在流感季節前往擠滿太多人的地方。

10. **shuffle** (*v.*) 拖著 (腳) 走 ⑥

· Movies often picture zombies **shuffling** down the road in groups.
電影經常描繪殭屍成群拖著腳走在路上。

11. **sway** (*v.*) 搖擺 ④

· The teens attending the school dance happily **swayed** their hips to the music.
參加舞會的青少年快樂地隨著音樂擺臀。

12. **misery** (*n.*) 悲慘 ③

· Joseph's life is a real **misery**. He lost his parents when he was a kid, and now his son has died of illness.
Joseph 的人生實屬悲慘。他年幼時失去了父母，現在他的兒子因病死亡。

13. **entertain** (*v.*) 使娛樂 ④

· Every night, the band would play at the subway station to **entertain** the passengers.
每天晚上，這個樂團會在地鐵站表演來娛樂乘客。

14. **audience** (*n.*) 觀眾 ③

· When the show was over, the **audience** gave the performers a standing ovation.
當演出結束時，觀眾對表演者起立鼓掌。

15. **popularity** (*n.*) 人氣 ④

· Short-form video apps have gained in **popularity** among teenagers nowadays.
短影音應用程式已在現今青少年中獲得人氣。

16. **talent** (*n.*) 才能 ③

· Jimmy really showed **talent** for guitar. He learned how to play it all by himself.
Jimmy 真的展現了吉他的才能。他全靠自己學會如何彈吉他。

17. **blend** (*v.*) 混和 ④

· Led Zeppelin was skilled at producing music that **blended** American blues with British folk music.
齊柏林飛船樂團擅長創作融合美國藍調和英國民謠的音樂。

18. **immigrant** (*n.*) 移民 ④

· Jane's grandparents were **immigrants** that moved to the United States in order to flee the Nazi regime.

Jane 的祖父母是為了逃離納粹政權而遷徙至美國的移民。

參考字彙

1. minstrel show (*n.*) 黑人劇團

慣用語和片語

1. **rob . . . of . . .** 搶奪 (某人/物)

· People of this country were **robbed of** their peace when the neighboring country invaded them.

這個國家的人民在鄰國入侵他們時被剝奪了和平。

2. **take notice of . . .** 注意…

· Activists hold demonstrations to urge the government to **take notice of** environmental issues.

激進分子舉行示威活動以敦促政府注意環境議題。

Note

- -

- -

- -

- -

- -

- -

- -

- -

- -

- -

- -

- -

- -

- -

Unit 4

The Strange Appeal of Boring Television

Warm-up Questions

1. What kind of TV show do you like?

2. Do you know what Slow TV is about?

3. Would a TV show that features only scenery attract you?

With rapid advances in technology, the pace of life keeps speeding up. It's even suggested our constant occupation with our electronic devices, our favorite apps, and the Internet is making it harder for people to pay attention to anything for more than a short time. We want variety. We want entertainment. We want what's new, colorful, and therefore exciting for us. What's more, we want it NOW!

❶ It may seem strange in times like these—when we seem to be less patient than ever—that people are turning to something more slow-paced for entertainment. ❷ Yet a new phenomenon called "Slow TV" is taking the world by storm. ❸ The concept emerged from Norway. ❹ Producers of this new brand of television program decided to throw the old <u>rule book</u> out the window, so to speak. ❺ They did away with conventions like spoken dialogue, cast members chosen for their good looks, and story lines building up to exciting climaxes. ❻ Meanwhile, they decided to stick with the idea of "reality TV"—a proven format that has enjoyed popularity in recent years.

The resulting programs feature hour after hour of people doing quite ordinary activities. Think fourteen hours of uninterrupted bird-watching or eighteen straight hours of fishing. Not your speed? How about a twelve-hour boat ride or a seven-hour journey by train through the snowy Norwegian countryside?

The producers have chosen a different way of telling stories—by letting viewers make them up themselves. The audience is shown scenes they can easily relate to, deeply rooted in their culture, and taken on a journey that gives them the feeling of being there. As viewers start noticing small details, it naturally prompts them to ask questions. Left on their own, they must make up stories to satisfy their curiosity, which engages their imaginations.

_____ 1. 請從下列 (A) 到 (F) 中，選出對 Slow TV 描述正確的選項。(多選題)

(A) Slow TV promotes classical movies and silent films.

(B) Slow TV encourages people to use their imaginations.

(C) Slow TV features latest TV programs with dramatic plot lines.

(D) Slow TV shows gorgeous men and women having conversations.

(E) Slow TV employs advanced technology to provide entertainment.

(F) Slow TV combines the idea of "reality TV" with ordinary activities.

2. Which word in the passage is closest in meaning to **"rule book"** in the second paragraph? (簡答)

_____

3. The sentences in paragraph 2 are numbered ❶ to ❻. Which sentence best indicates the author's intention to arouse the reader's curiosity about Slow TV? Write down the **NUMBER** of the sentence.

_____

_____ 4. Which of the following pictures best represents the scene of a typical Slow TV program? (單選)

(A)

(B)

(C)

(D)

重要字彙

1. **advance** (*n.*) 發展 ②
· **Advances** in communication technology over the past few decades have changed our way of living.
通訊科技過去數十年來的發展改變了我們的生活方式。

2. **constant** (*adj.*) 不停的 ③
· Miller still has **constant** nightmares about the rail accident he experienced a year ago.
Miller 仍不停夢到關於一年前遭遇火車事故的惡夢。

3. **occupation** (*n.*) 佔據 ④
· Steve's **occupation** with mobile games has taken a toll on his academic performance.
Steve 沉溺於手機遊戲而嚴重影響了他的學業表現。

4. **electronic** (*adj.*) 電子的 ③
· **Electronic** dance music is popular among younger generations today.
電子舞曲受到現今年輕世代的歡迎。

5. **device** (*n.*) 裝置 ④
· An AED is a portable medical **device** that can be operated by people without first-aid training.
自動體外心臟電擊去顫器是一種可攜式醫療裝置，沒受過急救訓練的人也能操作使用。

6. **variety** (*n.*) 多樣性 ③
· Taiwan is an island that has a wide **variety** of animals and plants owing to its unique geography.
由於獨特的地理條件，臺灣是一座動植物非常具有多樣性的島嶼。

7. **phenomenon** (*n.*) 現象 ④
· Meeting potential partners through dating apps is a **phenomenon** of modern romance.
透過約會應用程式來和潛在的伴侶相識，是現代戀情的一種現象。

8. **emerge** (*v.*) 出現 ④
· True heroes **emerge** only when the times call for them to save the day.
真正的英雄只有在時局需要時才會挺身而出。

9. **convention** (*n.*) 慣例 ④
· The **conventions** of what it means to be a man or a woman are now being challenged.
關於怎樣才算是一個男人或女人的傳統觀念現在正受到挑戰。

10. **cast** (*n.*) 演員陣容 ③
- This Hollywood Christmas movie features a **cast** that includes A-list actors and actresses.
  這部好萊塢聖誕電影的陣容包含多位知名男女演員。

11. **climax** (*n.*) 高潮 ⑥
- The **climax** of the concert was when the legendary band reunited and played several of their famous songs.
  當那個傳奇樂團重新合體，並演出多首他們的知名歌曲時，演唱會達到了高潮。

12. **proven** (*adj.*) 被證明的
- It is a **proven** fact that climate change is primarily caused by human activities.
  氣候變遷主要是人為活動造成的，這是已被證明的事實。

13. **format** (*n.*) (電視節目的) 形式 ⑤
- The TV-based **format** of comedy shows has been replaced by an on-demand **format** on streaming services.
  喜劇節目已從電視播放的形式改為在串流平臺上隨選播出。

14. **feature** (*v.*) 以…為特色 ②
- Our hotel **features** a beautiful sea view and a private beach where you can enjoy uninterrupted quality time.
  本旅館的特色包括美麗的海景，還有可以不受干擾享受優質時光的私人海灘。

15. **prompt** (*v.*) 促使 ④
- The fear of being rejected **prompted** Jeremy to act weirdly around the person he liked.
  對於遭到拒絕的憂慮促使 Jeremy 在喜歡的人身邊變得舉止怪異。

16. **engage** (*v.*) 引起 ③
- Lucy **engaged** the baby's interest with a teddy bear, which made the baby giggle.
  Lucy 用泰迪熊引起小寶寶的興趣，逗得寶寶咯咯發笑。

參考字彙

1. slow-paced (*adj.*) 步調緩慢的
2. uninterrupted (*adj.*) 不間斷的

慣用語和片語

1. **stick with** . . . 繼續做⋯
· Despite great difficulties, we decided to **stick with** our original plan and finished the project.
即使遭遇很大的困難，我們還是決定繼續維持原本的安排，完成了這個企劃。

2. **relate to** . . . 認同
· Asian children can easily **relate to** this movie because most of the main characters are Chinese-American.
因為本片的主要角色多為美籍華人，亞裔的兒童很容易就能產生認同。

Note

Unit 5

The Two Faces of Wildfires

Warm-up Questions

1. What are wildfires? How do they happen?

2. What kinds of damage can wildfires cause?

3. What kinds of positive effects can wildfires bring?

Wildfires, whether caused by humans or sparked by lightning strikes, are usually referred to as disasters. There is a good reason for this: besides trees, wildfires consume everything in their path, including homes and businesses. They can result in the loss of life and property, causing grief and millions of dollars of damage. They are incredibly expensive and dangerous to fight, and the damage they cause persists, too. Houses can be rebuilt, but it typically takes a couple of decades for a forest area scarred by the fire to be covered by trees again. Of course, the destruction of mature trees which otherwise could have been chopped down for lumber can be understood in terms of the economic cost. On the other hand, the elimination of the forest can also mean the loss of a scenic place for outdoor tourism, recreation, and leisure. Either way, forests are precious natural resources, and wildfires destroy them.

Despite all this, it can't be denied that wildfires play an important role in nature. For one thing, forest fires kill insects which threaten trees, like the emerald ash borer, a kind of beetle. Without fires to keep the population of emerald ash borers in check, the species would spread further and faster, allowing the destruction they cause to ash trees to be even more widespread.

Moreover, wildfires clear the thick layer of treetops over the forest, and the leaves and branches that cover the forest floor. Once mature trees are eliminated, sunlight can reach seeds and immature trees on the forest floor, giving them an opportunity to grow up. This gives new species—so-called "pioneer plants"—a chance to establish themselves where other tree species had previously dominated.

One thing is for certain: as hot, dry weather conditions continue, and human towns and cities stretch further and further into natural areas, wildfires will continue to do what they do—good and bad—year after year.

1. 請根據選文內容，從第二段和第三段各選出一個單詞 (word)，分別填入下列兩句的空格，並視語法需要作適當的字形變化，使句子語意完整、語法正確，且符合全文文意。(填空)

Without wildfires, the emerald ash borers would multiply and (A) ＿＿＿＿＿＿＿ vast areas of the forest.

Wildfires could end the (B) ＿＿＿＿＿＿＿ of mature trees in a forest, and give space for new species of trees to grow.

＿＿＿＿ 2. According to the passage, which of the following best describes what emerald ash borers do to the trees? (單選)

(A) They help to clear the thick layer of the treetops.

(B) They serve as a good research topic on tree species.

(C) They disturb the flow of nutrients and water in the trees.

(D) They pose a threat to other insects feeding on tree leaves.

3–6. "..., wildfires will continue to do what they do—good and bad—year after year."

From (A) to (D) below, put the statements in the categories "good/bad" according to the passage. (單選)

(A) Wildfires burn down mature trees and result in lumber loss.

(B) Wildfires pollute the water sources and cause animal deaths.

(C) Wildfires eliminate mature trees, allowing pioneer species to grow.

(D) Wildfires scar the forest which could have been used for leisure activities.

(E) Wildfires clear the forest ground, making space for humans to build houses.

(F) Wildfires destroy insects which otherwise could have been more widespread.

good	3. ＿＿＿＿ 4. ＿＿＿＿
bad	5. ＿＿＿＿ 6. ＿＿＿＿

重要字彙

1. **spark** (*v.*) 引發 ④
   · The recent border conflicts have **sparked** an all-out war between the two countries.
   近來的邊境衝突引發了兩國之間的全面戰爭。

2. **lightning** (*n.*) 閃電 ③
   · A bolt of **lightning** struck the clock tower and damaged its structure.
   一道閃電擊中鐘塔，導致其結構受損。

3. **consume** (*v.*) 燒毀 ④
   · Fire **consumed** everyone in that building. No one survived.
   大火吞噬了那棟屋子裡的每一個人。沒有人生還。

4. **property** (*n.*) 財產 ③
   · Since the historic building is private **property**, its owner has the final word on whether it is to be preserved.
   既然這棟歷史建築是私人財產，屋主對於是否保存它有最後的決定權。

5. **grief** (*n.*) 悲痛 ④
   · Ashley finds it difficult to move on from the **grief** of losing his child.
   Ashley 認為要走出喪子之痛很困難。

6. **incredibly** (*adv.*) 極為 ④
   · Climbing Mount Everest is considered an **incredibly** dangerous task. People have lost their lives when making the climb.
   攀爬聖母峰被認為是一項極為危險的任務。人們曾在攻頂途中失去了性命。

7. **persist** (*v.*) 持續存留 ⑤
   · The trauma of physical or emotional abuse, if not properly resolved, tends to **persist**.
   身體或情感虐待的創傷如果沒有適當解決，很可能會持續留存下來。

8. **typically** (*adv.*) 通常
   · Rice is **typically** grown on a large scale in East Asian and Southeast Asian countries.
   水稻在東亞和東南亞國家通常會大規模種植。

9. **scar** (*v.*) 損傷 ⑤
   · Kate was mentally **scarred** by the insult from her parents.
   來自父母的羞辱讓 Kate 精神受創。

10. **destruction** (*n.*) 破壞 ④
- The **destruction** of the power facilities by enemy missiles has left this country suffering during winter.
敵方導彈對電力設施的破壞讓這個國家在冬天十分難熬。

11. **otherwise** (*adv.*) 原本 ④
- Under Jessie's careful inspections, several mistakes that might **otherwise** have been missed were spotted.
在 Jessie 的仔細檢查下，幾個原本會漏掉的錯誤都被抓出來了。

12. **economic** (*adj.*) 經濟上的 ④
- After COVID-19 became a pandemic, it triggered a global **economic** recession because the whole world was in lockdown.
新冠肺炎在大流行之後導致了全球性的經濟衰退，因為全世界都處於封鎖狀態。

13. **threaten** (*v.*) 威脅 ③
- Kylo **threatened** to destroy all that Rey held dear if she did not do what she was told.
Kylo 威脅 Rey，如果不照她所被交代的去做，就要摧毀她所珍惜的一切。

14. **widespread** (*adj.*) 廣布的 ⑤
- Child abuse is more common and **widespread** than people think it is.
對兒童的虐待比人們認為的更常見，也發生得更廣泛。

15. **eliminate** (*v.*) 消滅 ④
- Despite the government's efforts, this invasive species is still far from being completely **eliminated**.
即便政府已有所努力，距離這種入侵物種遭到完全消滅，還有很長的路要走。

16. **pioneer** (*n.*) 先驅者 ④
- The United States and Russia were the **pioneers** in space exploration.
美國和俄羅斯是太空探索的先驅。

17. **establish** (*v.*) 立足 ④
- Robert has **established** his position in the music industry with his talent and hard work.
Robert 藉著才華和努力，在音樂界取得了一席之地。

18. **dominate** (*v.*) 支配 ④
- Before dinosaurs were wiped out, they had **dominated** the Earth for millions of years.
在恐龍滅絕之前，牠們曾支配地球達數百萬年之久。

參考字彙

1. lumber (*n.*) 木材

慣用語和片語

1. **keep . . . in check** 抑制…

· Social distancing, testing, and quarantine must be carried out to **keep** the number of infections **in check**.

保持社交距離、篩檢以及隔離都必須做到，才能抑制染病的人數。

Note

- -

- -

- -

- -

- -

- -

- -

- -

- -

- -

- -

- -

- -

- -

Unit 6

Worrying About Numbers: The Common Problem of Math Anxiety

Warm-up Questions

1. Do you feel anxious about math? Why?

2. What factors might contribute to math anxiety?

3. What can be done to overcome math anxiety?

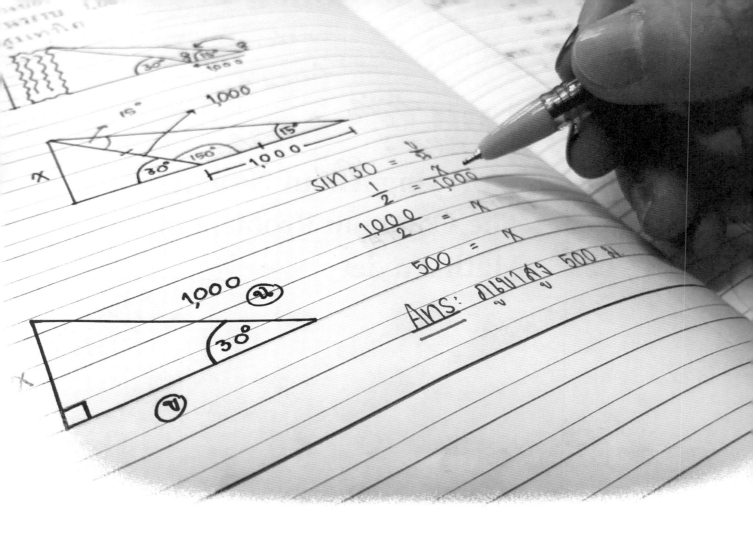

There is a myth that boys are better at math than girls, but this is not true. What is true is that a lot of boys and girls, and men and women too, worry about math and feel nervous and uncomfortable when they have to do it.

Picture this scene: students sit in class waiting to take a math test. They can feel their hearts beating in their chests. Their hands are shaking and their palms are covered in a lot of sweat. They are worried they will fail, even though they have studied hard and practiced solving countless math problems. It is hard—almost impossible really—to concentrate, which is what they need to do most to pass the test successfully.

Does this sound familiar? If so, you are not alone. In fact, it is estimated that about 20 percent of people suffer from symptoms like these as part of a condition experts call "math anxiety."

Math anxiety is based on fear of failure. The self-doubt often starts early in one's academic career. In elementary school, it is not uncommon for math to be presented to students as something that is, by its very nature, challenging and difficult. This creates an expectation in young minds. What's more, there is often pressure on learners to do things quickly—like being able to memorize multiplication tables or mathematical formulas and recite them on demand. Compounding the problem, some cultures associate math smarts with overall intelligence. This perception makes students who are not strong on math feel they are somehow inadequate.

Fortunately, specialists in educational psychology are quick to assure us that math anxiety can be overcome. For one thing, parents and teachers can try to make math less frightening and avoid putting too much pressure on kids. Students themselves can try relaxation techniques, like deep breathing exercises, to calm their nerves. They can also write down their worries, since doing this helps to clarify the exact cause of them, and can make their anxiety less overwhelming.

_____ 1. 請從下列 (A) 到 (F) 中，選出本文所提供的資訊有哪些。(多選題)

(A) Devising a test to measure math ability.

(B) Applying math skills to real-life situations.

(C) Identifying the symptoms of math anxiety.

(D) Conducting a survey to estimate math anxiety.

(E) Comparing boys' math scores with those of girls'.

(F) Providing advice on easing worries about math learning.

2. Which word in the fourth paragraph means "making a difficult situation worse"? (簡答)

_____

3. Fill in the blanks with the information contained in the passage about math anxiety.
(填表題)

Problem: math anxiety

Solutions	
parents and teachers	• try to make math less frightening • (A) _____
students	• try relaxation techniques • (B) _____

重要字彙

1. **myth** (*n.*) 迷思 ⑤
· A team of experts put this long-held **myth** to the test with experiments.
專家小組透過實驗來檢證這個長久存在的迷思。

2. **palm** (*n.*) 手掌 ③
· Lela carefully held the bird with a broken wing in the **palm** of her hand as she took it to the vet.
Lela 小心地將翅膀折斷的鳥兒捧在掌心，帶去給獸醫。

3. **concentrate** (*v.*) 專心 ④
· Some people find it hard to **concentrate** in the library because it's just too quiet.
有些人覺得圖書館裡很難專心，因為裡頭太安靜了。

4. **estimate** (*v.*) 估計 ④
· The WHO **estimates** that by the end of the year, 70% of the world's population will be infected.
世界衛生組織估計到了年底，全世界百分之七十的人口都會被感染。

5. **symptom** (*n.*) 症狀 ⑤
· **Symptoms** of flu include sore throats, fever, muscle aches, and fatigue.
流感的症狀包含喉嚨痛、發燒、肌肉酸痛以及疲倦。

6. **anxiety** (*n.*) 焦慮 ④
· There has been a growing **anxiety** over the threat of a potential energy crisis caused by the war in Eastern Europe.
面對東歐戰事可能導致能源危機的威脅，人們的焦慮日益增加。

7. **academic** (*adj.*) 學業的 ④
· Andy's excellent **academic** performance has made him the talk of the school.
Andy 傑出的學業表現讓他成為校內的話題人物。

8. **challenging** (*adj.*) 具挑戰性的
· Staying in a closed room without any contact with the outside world has proven extremely **challenging** for people.
待在封閉的房間裡、與外界隔絕一切接觸，事實證明這對人類來說是極具挑戰性的。

9. **formula** (*n.*) 【數】公式 ④
- Though never receiving any formal education, Will can understand these **formulas** with ease.
  雖然 Will 未曾受過任何正式教育，他卻可以輕易地理解這些公式。

10. **recite** (*v.*) 背誦 ⑤
- Students in this school have to **recite** a great number of poems and passages in school.
  這所學校的學生在學校必須背誦許多詩詞語句。

11. **intelligence** (*n.*) 智慧 ④
- Emotional maturity is important when determining a person's **intelligence**.
  判定一個人的智慧時，情緒的成熟度是重要的考量。

12. **perception** (*n.*) 觀念 ⑤
- Public **perception** of mental health issues has been changing; more and more people are willing to talk about it now.
  大眾對心理健康問題的觀念已經在改變了；現在有越來越多人願意開口談論它。

13. **inadequate** (*adj.*) 不夠格的
- Jade felt very much **inadequate** as she was suddenly promoted to store manager.
  Jade 突然被拔擢為店長時，她覺得自己實在沒有那個資格。

  adequate (*adj.*) 合格的 ④
- The quality of the assignment that Jude just handed in is barely **adequate**.
  Jude 剛剛交來的作業勉強及格。

14. **nerves** (*n.*) 焦躁
- When Collins starts to pace back and forth, you know that his **nerves** are on edge.
  當 Collins 開始來回踱步，你就知道他正處於焦躁狀態。

15. **clarify** (*v.*) 釐清 ④
- Every time I get stuck on writing my paper, I go for a walk; it helps me **clarify** my thoughts.
  每當我寫論文卡住時，我就會去散散步；這樣有助我釐清思緒。

16. **overwhelming** (*adj.*) 難以忍受的
- An **overwhelming** feeling of loss hit Percy after his partner broke up with him.
  Percy 在伴侶和他分手後，感受到一陣難以忍受的失落。

參考字彙

1. multiplication table (*n.*) 乘法表

慣用語和片語

1. **suffer from . . .** 受⋯之苦
   · Taiwan has **suffered from** water shortage in recent years as a result of changes in regional climate patterns.
   近年臺灣因區域氣候模式的改變而遭受缺水之苦。

2. **on demand** 一經要求
   · With streaming services, you can watch all kinds of films and TV shows **on demand**.
   透過串流服務，你可以隨選即看各種影片和電視節目。

3. **associate . . . with . . .** 把⋯和⋯聯繫在一起
   · People often **associate** Christmas **with** home, family values, and the spirit of giving.
   人們經常將聖誕節與家庭、家庭價值以及給予的精神聯繫在一起。

Note

Unit 7

The New Intelligence Requires Distinguishing Facts from Opinions

Warm-up Questions

1. What do you know about fake news?

2. How can facts be distinguished from opinions?

3. Do you know how to fact-check a piece of information?

Much has been made of so-called "fake news," and a lot of people will suggest you can't trust anything you hear or read these days. With computers, mobile devices, and Internet access, everyone has uninterrupted access to almost unlimited amounts of all kinds of information. In the modern era, it could be argued that a big part of what constitutes intelligence is the ability to distinguish facts from opinions.

Facts are statements that are supported by evidence. In other words, they can be checked and proved to be correct. Facts are objective, which means any sensible person would be satisfied a fact is true after reviewing statistics or scientific studies.

Unlike facts, opinions cannot be proved to be true or false because they're based on personal beliefs, feelings, or judgments. Opinions, however, can be backed up or supported by evidence if a person does research to uncover facts that support his or her feelings or beliefs.

When it comes to sorting out what is a fact and what is an opinion, there are some key words to watch for. For example, when people use value words like "best," "better," and "worst," it is a good clue that what's being said is an opinion. The word "should" is also an indicator that you are hearing someone's personal point of view. When people speak in absolute terms using "always" and "never," what follows is often an opinion, too.

Most media these days is not exactly what could be called neutral. In other words, media channels will seek to slant the facts they present to reflect certain opinions or advance particular agendas. For example, a television network may make one political party look good at the expense of another, by reporting favorable stories about the former, and giving negative coverage to the latter. Such a network could be described as having a "pro-government" or "anti-government" outlook, depending on the political leanings of its owners.

Keep this in mind and remember: real intelligence means distinguishing facts from opinions.

_____ 1. Which of the following can be inferred from this passage? (單選)

    (A) People tend to choose media channels that report no fake news.

    (B) A person who can tell facts from opinions is of great intelligence.

    (C) The Internet seldom provides accurate statistics and scientific studies.

    (D) It is suggested that most information in the modern era are fake news.

2. Which word in the passage means "to give information to support a particular opinion"? (簡答)

_____

3. 根據本文說明關於 facts 和 opinions 所述的特性，請將下列尚未填入表格的選項進行分類，屬於 fact statement，填入 Facts 欄位；屬於 opinion statement，填入 Opinions 欄位。(填表題)

(A) Movies without intense action scenes are always boring.

(B) Japan is considered one of the best countries in the world.

(C) Fossil evidence suggests that some dinosaurs had feathers.

(D) The greatest president of the United States is Barack Obama.

(E) Studies reveal the connection between smoking and lung cancer.

(F) Statistics show that Taiwan's population is around twenty-three million.

Facts	Opinions
• _____ • E • F	• A • _____ • _____

重要字彙

1. **access** (*n.*) 【電腦】存取 ④
   · Subscribed members will have **access** to our exclusive content.
   有訂閱的會員將能存取我們的專屬內容。

2. **constitute** (*v.*) 構成 ④
   · Extreme weather events triggered by climate change **constitute** a threat to human survival.
   氣候變遷引發的極端天氣事件對於人類生存構成了威脅。

3. **distinguish** (*v.*) 辨別 ④
   · In the movie, the main characters find themselves unable to **distinguish** dreams from reality.
   在該片中，主角們發現自己無法分辨夢境與真實。

4. **evidence** (*n.*) 證據 ④
   · Archeological **evidence** suggests that this ancient civilization had the ability to sail on the sea.
   考古證據顯示這個古文明擁有航海的能力。

5. **objective** (*adj.*) 客觀的 ④
   · Before **objective** evidence is found, no one can suggest that a person is guilty.
   在找到客觀證據之前，沒有人可以推定一個人有罪。

6. **sensible** (*adj.*) 明智的 ③
   · Mariah made the **sensible** choice to leave when her partner became too controlling.
   Mariah 在伴侶變得控制慾太強之前就抽身是明智的選擇。

7. **statistics** (*n.*) 統計數字 ④
   · **Statistics** show that the number of road traffic deaths in Taiwan is among the highest in developed countries.
   統計數字顯示臺灣道路交通的死亡人數在已開發國家中名列前茅。

8. **judgment** (*n.*) 評斷 ②
   · People tend to make **judgments** based on their past experience.
   人們傾向根據過往的經驗來做出評斷。

9. **uncover** (*v.*) 發掘 ⑤

· Harry **uncovered** the truth about who really betrayed his parents.
  Harry 發現了究竟是誰背叛了他父母的真相。

10. **absolute** (*adj.*) 斷然的 ④

· Always doubt when you hear someone making an **absolute** claim about something.
  當你聽到有人對某事提出斷然的主張，永遠要心存懷疑。

11. **neutral** (*adj.*) 中立的 ⑤

· Remaining **neutral** did not help Belgium escape the invasion of Nazi Germany.
  保持中立無助於比利時避免納粹德國的侵略。

12. **agenda** (*n.*) 議題 ⑤

· The **agenda** of this conference is "gender, space, and COVID-19."
  這場研討會的議題是「性別、空間與新冠肺炎」。

13. **favorable** (*adj.*) 有利的 ④

· Coraline only presents information that is **favorable** to her image.
  Coraline 只會呈現對自己形象有利的資訊。

14. **coverage** (*n.*) 新聞報導 ⑤

· Real-time news **coverage** has changed the way people perceive war.
  即時新聞報導改變了人們認知戰爭的方式。

15. **outlook** (*n.*) 觀點 ⑥

· The circumstances of the world today have led younger generations to develop a rather gloomy **outlook** on their future.
  今日的世界局勢讓年輕世代對於未來產生了相當悲觀的看法。

16. **leaning** (*n.*) 傾向

· Jordan has a **leaning** toward social thriller films.
  Jordan 對社會驚悚片有所偏好。

參考字彙

1. indicator (*n.*) 指標
2. slant (*v.*) 偏頗報導

慣用語和片語

1. **sort out** 將⋯分類
· Good time management means being able to **sort out** one's priorities.
良好的時間管理意謂著能夠區分事情的輕重緩急。

2. **at the expense of . . .** 犧牲
· It is not worthy of pursuing excellence **at the expense of** physical or mental well-being.
為了追求卓越而犧牲身體或心理的健康是很不值得的。

Note

- -

- -

- -

- -

- -

- -

- -

- -

- -

- -

- -

- -

- -

- -

- -

Unit 8

An Instantly Recognizable Adventurer: Tintin

Warm-up Questions

1. Do you have a favorite cartoon character?

2. What are the stories of Tintin usually about?

3. Can you describe the appearance of Tintin?

Tintin is a cartoon character created by the Belgian artist Hergé. He first appeared in a comic series bearing his name in the 1940s, and has been beloved by generations of fans ever since. Readers admire his heroic deeds, bravery, and intelligence that make it possible for him to accomplish his dangerous missions.

In his job as a reporter, Tintin often uncovers the crimes of the villains. His adventures take him around the world—from the humid jungles of the Congo and the Pyramids of Egypt in Africa to the heights of the Himalayas in Asia—and beyond. One early work in the series, *Red Rackham's Treasure*, sees our hero navigating deep beneath the sea in a shark-shaped submarine. *Explorers on the Moon* sees his journey into space with his astronaut friends aboard a rocket ship. A born adventurer, he's equally comfortable zooming around by airplane, helicopter, boat, train, race car, or motorcycle.

Tintin looks like a teenage boy. He's thin and not tall, with light brown hair cut short. One distinctive lock of hair in front is swept upward over his forehead like a little wave. His clothes seldom change—unless he's in disguise to hide his identity or dressed for a specific purpose. He usually wears a light blue, long-sleeved sweater over a white dress shirt with a collar, along with brown pants tucked into white socks. When the weather calls for it, he wears a long brown trench coat with the collar turned up. His faithful little white dog, Snowy, is always by his side. Tintin and Snowy, together with other friends, have been through a lot and have saved each other's lives on many occasions in the course of their adventures.

Despite his youthful appearance and his thin figure, Tintin is physically strong and fast. He's also fearless, and regularly puts himself in harm's way to solve mysteries, prevent crimes, and catch criminals. He's smart, skilled at planning, and good-hearted. He'll do anything he can to help his friends.

_____ 1. 請從下列 (A) 到 (F) 中，選出文章對 Tintin 的描述都正確的選項。(多選題)

(A) Tintin's adventures are based on true stories.

(B) Tintin sets off on journeys to seek fortune and fame.

(C) Tintin has a sharp intellect and can defend himself and his friends.

(D) Tintin is initially a weak character, but later evolves and becomes heroic.

(E) Tintin is involved in dangerous cases in which he stops crimes successfully.

(F) Tintin and Snowy travel through several countries in pursuit of true friends.

_____ 2. Which of the following figures best represents Tintin's typical image? (單選)

(A) 　　　　(B)

(C) 　　　　(D)

3. 請根據選文內容，從第一段及第三段中各選出一個單詞 (word)，分別填入下列兩句的空格，並視語法需要作適當的字形變化，使句子語意完整、語法正確，且符合全文文意。(填空)

Tintin is brave and intelligent enough to stop criminal acts and succeed in (A) _____ all kinds of missions.

Being a master of (B) _____, Tintin is able to travel around without being recognized by anyone who might know him.

重要字彙

1. **bear** (*v.*) 帶有 ①
· The boy **bears** a scar in the shape of a lightning bolt on his forehead.
那個男孩的額頭上有一道閃電形狀的疤痕。

2. **heroic** (*adj.*) 英勇的 ⑥
· John was rewarded the Medal of Honor for his **heroic** actions during the battle.
John 因他在戰場上的英勇行為而獲頒榮譽勳章。

3. **deed** (*n.*) 行為 ③
· Hanna does a lot of good **deeds**, such as raising money for people in need.
Hanna 做了很多好事，比如說為貧困的人募款。

4. **bravery** (*n.*) 勇氣 ③
· Fighting cancer requires **bravery**, for one has to undergo a series of painful treatments.
與癌症搏鬥需要勇氣，因為必須接受一連串痛苦的治療。

5. **accomplish** (*v.*) 完成 ④
· I'm pleased that I've **accomplished** all the goals I set for the year.
我很高興自己完成了今年設下的全數目標。

6. **mission** (*n.*) 任務 ③
· Your **mission**, should you choose to accept it, is to eliminate the terrorists and save the hostages.
你的任務，若你選擇接受的話，是消滅恐怖分子並且救出人質。

7. **villain** (*n.*) 壞人 ⑥
· *Joker* is a movie about the backstory of a DC Comics **villain**.
《小丑》是一部講述 DC 漫畫反派角色背景故事的電影。

8. **navigate** (*v.*) 航行 ⑥
· Back in the old days, sailors had to **navigate** their way using compasses and stars.
在過往的時代，水手得靠羅盤和星象來導航。

9. **submarine** (*n.*) 潛水艇 ④
· Scientists operate an unmanned **submarine** to explore the deep sea.
科學家操縱無人潛水艇來探索深海。

10. astronaut (*n.*) 太空人 ⑥

· American **astronauts** were the first men that walked on the surface of the Moon.
美國的太空人是首批在月球表面行走的人類。

11. zoom (*v.*) 快速移動 ⑥

· George **zoomed** from Taipei to Kaohsiung and back within a single day.
George 在一天之內快速往返臺北高雄兩地。

12. distinctive (*adj.*) 特別的 ⑤

· This blend of tobacco has a **distinctive** fruity scent.
這種菸草配方有種獨特的水果香氣。

13. disguise (*n.*) 偽裝 ④

· Holmes wore a fake beard and mustache as a **disguise** so that he could fool his enemies.
Holmes 戴上假鬍鬚當作偽裝，以便愚弄他的敵人。

14. collar (*n.*) 衣領 ③

· Captain Miller grabbed his man by the **collar** and commanded him to follow orders.
Miller 上尉揪住部下的衣領，命令他服從指示。

15. tuck (*v.*) 把…塞進 ⑥

· While the school authority requires students to **tuck** in their uniform shirts, most of them do not act accordingly.
雖然校方規定學生要把制服上衣紮好，但多數人並沒有照做。

16. faithful (*adj.*) 忠實的 ④

· Stevens was a **faithful** servant to his mistress; he defended her while no one else did.
Stevens 是他女主人的忠實僕人；唯有他一人為她辯護。

17. occasion (*n.*) 時候 ③

· Living in Hollywood, I have bumped into movie stars on several **occasions**.
我因為住在好萊塢，有時候會碰見電影明星。

18. mystery (*n.*) 謎團 ③

· How this aircraft accident happened remains a **mystery** to this day.
這起航空事故的起因至今仍是未解之謎。

19. **criminal** (*n.*) 罪犯 ③

· The police have arrested a group of **criminals** that were involved in drug dealing.
警方逮捕了一群從事毒品買賣的罪犯。

◯◯ 參考字彙

1. trench coat (*n.*) 風衣

Note

....

....

....

....

....

....

....

....

....

....

....

....

....

....

Unit 9

The Secret to Living a Good Life

Warm-up Questions

1. What makes a good life to you?

2. What do you do to keep your relationship close?

3. How are relationships linked with health?

To attempt to answer the question of "What Makes a Good Life?", a long-term Harvard University study has tracked seven hundred and twenty-four subjects over the course of seventy-five years, from adolescence to old age. The study has concluded that strong social connections with family, friends, and one's community lead to more happiness, better physical health, and longer life. As a result, the study argues that people should put effort into building and maintaining such relationships.

When it comes to our relationships, evidence suggests quality is more important than quantity. In other words, it doesn't matter so much if one has many friends or just a few. The closeness of the friendships is what counts most, so it's arguably better to have a few close friends than many acquaintances. The study found those people who were most satisfied with their relationships at age fifty were most likely to be healthy at eighty.

Good relationships with people we care about seem to have a positive effect on our health, but the opposite is also true: relationships that are filled with conflict harm our health. Therefore, we should do what is necessary to maintain bonds and renew or strengthen relationships that have become strained or weakened. We can strive to keep relationships vital and meaningful by engaging in new activities. Beyond the physical, good relationships protect our brains, helping our memories stay sharper and longer. Loneliness, in contrast, is toxic. Isolation leads to less happiness, declining health, and shorter life.

❶ Human beings tend to assume that accumulating wealth and social status can ultimately guarantee a good and happy life. ❷ However, the study provides abundant evidence that overrules such general belief. ❸ We can change our ways of thinking and make the right decisions to pursue what it really means to have a good and happy life. ❹ Therefore, to have a good life, we should actively try to make friends and spend more time with people we care about instead of staring at computers and smartphones, becoming more and more isolated.

_____ 1. 請從下列 (A) 到 (F) 中，選出對文章提及之研究所述正確的選項。(多選題)

(A) People become healthier if they have more friends.

(B) The study provides ideas about how we can lead a good life.

(C) Conflicts between family members lead to closer family bonds.

(D) The study confirms that high achievements guarantee happiness.

(E) People can be satisfied and healthier by building good relationships.

(F) People gain better memories when they spend more time on computers.

_____ 2. According to the passage, which of the following best describes the author's attitude towards the study? (單選)

(A) Approving.　　(B) Doubtful.　　(C) Humorous.　　(D) Sarcastic.

3. The sentences in paragraph 4 are numbered ❶ to ❹. Which sentence best indicates the author's intention to provide do's and don'ts for achieving a good life? Write down the **NUMBER** of the sentence.

_____

_____ 4. According to the following social media posts, who is most likely to have a good life? (單選)

Wilson	I don't know why my friends turned down my birthday party invitation. It doesn't make any sense.

Jessie	My classmates and I seldom talk to each other now. But it's OK. I'm used to it already.

David	Gosh, doing those club activities is so tiring. Do I have to do all of this? Just leave me alone.

Betty	I got free tickets to tomorrow's concert from my friend. You're welcome to go with me. Message me if you're interested.

(A) Wilson.　　(B) Jessie.　　(C) David.　　(D) Betty.

重要字彙

1. **attempt** (*v.*) 嘗試 ②
   · Rose **attempted** to call for help, but she was too weak to make her voice heard.
   Rose 試圖求援，但因為她太虛弱了，沒人聽到她的聲音。

2. **subject** (*n.*) 研究對象 ①
   · In the end, **subjects** of the experiment were all getting sick, so the researchers had to shut it down.
   到了最後，所有研究對象全都感到不適，研究人員只好中止實驗。

3. **adolescence** (*n.*) 青少年期 ⑥
   · For many, their **adolescence** was defined by stress and anxiety.
   對許多人來說，壓力和焦慮一語道盡了他們的青春期。

4. **arguably** (*adv.*) 可以認為
   · David Bowie was **arguably** one of the best pop music artists in the 20th century.
   大衛鮑伊可說是二十世紀最優秀的流行樂手之一。

5. **acquaintance** (*n.*) 相識的人 ④
   · James and I are business **acquaintances**; we do not have a relationship outside of work.
   我和 James 只是業務上相識；我們在工作之外並沒有來往。

6. **bond** (*n.*) 聯結 ④
   · Tribes in the North forged a **bond** and fought the evil in the South together.
   北方的部落締結聯盟，共同對抗南方的邪惡勢力。

7. **renew** (*v.*) 更新 ④
   · We should **renew** this project and make it more appealing to today's generation.
   我們應該更新這個企劃，讓它對當今的世代更具吸引力。

8. **strengthen** (*v.*) 強化 ④
   · Soldiers **strengthened** their defense in anticipation of another wave of attack.
   士兵們加強防衛，為下一波攻勢做好準備。

9. **strained** (*adj.*) 緊張的

· There was a **strained** atmosphere at the dinner table; a fight might break out at any minute.

餐桌上有種緊張的氣氛；隨時可能會爆發衝突。

strain (*v.*) 使緊繃 ⑤

· A sudden surge of infection has **strained** hospitals around the country to their limit.

疫情突然加劇，讓全國醫院的負載量大為吃緊。

10. **strive** (*v.*) 努力 ④

· Our community **strives** to create a friendly environment to people of all backgrounds.

我們社區致力打造一個對所有背景的人都友善的環境。

11. **vital** (*adj.*) 有生氣的 ④

· Eating healthily, exercising regularly, and getting enough sleep will keep you young and **vital**.

健康的飲食、規律的運動，再加上充足的睡眠，能夠讓你保持年輕有活力。

12. **toxic** (*adj.*) 有害的 ⑤

· Nowadays, people have become better able to recognize **toxic** traits in relationships.

現今的人們已經較能察覺情感關係中有害的跡象。

13. **isolation** (*n.*) 孤立 ④

· Modern urban life is often characterized by a sense of **isolation**.

孤立的感受是現代城市生活常見的特徵。

14. **declining** (*adj.*) 衰退的

· Gloomy economic prospects and worsening environmental conditions contribute to **declining** birth rates.

黯淡的經濟前景以及惡化的環境條件導致生育率衰退。

decline (*v.*) 衰退 ⑤

· The population of leopard cats has rapidly **declined** as a result of human activities.

石虎的族群數量因為人為活動的關係急遽衰退。

15. **accumulate** (*v.*) 累積 ⑥

· Scientists still do not know how micro-plastics **accumulated** in the body will affect humans.

科學家仍不清楚在體內累積的塑膠微粒會對人類產生怎樣的影響。

16. **status** (*n.*) 地位 ④

· A higher social-economic **status** does not necessarily lead to good moral character.

較高的社會經濟地位並不必然導致良好的道德品格。

17. **ultimately** (*adv.*) 最終地

· **Ultimately**, all that lives will fade away and become a memory of the past.

最終，所有的生命都會消逝，成為過往的記憶。

18. **abundant** (*adj.*) 充足的 ⑤

· Here we have an **abundant** supply of soft drinks and snacks, so please feel free to enjoy yourselves.

我們這裡的軟性飲料和零食供應充足，所以請別客氣，盡情享用。

19. **pursue** (*v.*) 追求 ④

· Instead of wealth and fame, one should **pursue** a life of physical and emotional wellness.

一個人應該追求身心健康的生活，而非財富和名譽。

慣用語和片語

1. **put effort into** . . . 努力…

· Lately, the local authorities has **put effort into** conserving Japanese-era historic sites.

近來，地方當局努力保存日本時代的古蹟。

2. **engage in** . . . 從事…

· Daisy **engages in** voluntary work to assist the needy whenever she has time.

Daisy 只要有時間就會從事志工服務，協助困苦的人。

Note

Unit 10

What Happens to All Those Plastic Bottles Once We Dispose of Them?

Warm-up Questions

1. Have you ever visited a recovery facility?

2. Why do recovery facilities favor certain materials?

3. What are the ways for recycled plastic to be reused?

Most people today have recognized the importance of separating recyclable materials from trash. If we fail to take this step, the huge volume of garbage we produce will eventually overwhelm our capacity to deal with it. So it's common practice to deposit a single-use plastic bottle in a nearby recycling can once we finish drinking it. We feel like we have done our part, as far as protecting the environment goes. But what happens next?

First, the can is emptied and the contents are taken away by a truck to a materials recovery facility. This is often done by government workers, but contracts may be awarded to private companies to look after collection. At the recovery facility, the materials are sorted to see what can be used again. The basis for making the decision is purely a financial one. Recycling is a business, and as a rule, only materials that can be sold for a profit are selected. The rest are discarded because they have no resale value. The sorting process sees materials pass on conveyer belts through a series of metal detectors, magnets, tumbling machines, and human workers.

The so-called "PET plastic" used to make most bottles meets the value requirement, so empty PET bottles are tossed by the thousands into huge piles. Cranes then pick them up with giant claws, or mechanical loaders scoop them up with their shovels. They're dumped into machines that crush them flat and compact them into big cubes weighing up to a ton. These cubes are sold and taken away to recycling facilities.

Next, the cubes are broken apart, and green and clear plastic is separated by lasers that shine beams of light through them. Crushed bottles are cleaned with soap and heated so labels and caps fall off. Then, machines grind them into small flakes which are again washed, dried, and heated. These flakes can be turned into fabric, carpets, and even bottles, extending the life cycle of plastic.

_____ 1. 請從下列 (A) 到 (F) 中，選出對 plastic bottles 描述正確的選項。(多選題)

(A) Humans lack the capacity to process plastic bottles.

(B) PET bottles are the plastic we can recycle to make profits.

(C) All plastic bottles collected for recycling get recycled and reused.

(D) Plastic bottles in the can are later broken apart by human workers.

(E) Private recycling companies are usually funded by the government.

(F) Clean and green plastic is utilized as raw material for making fabrics.

2. What are "**these cubes**" in the third paragraph mainly made of? (簡答)

_____

3. 請根據選文內容，從第二段選出適當的字彙或詞組，分別填入下列流程圖中的兩個空格，且符合全文文意。(填空)

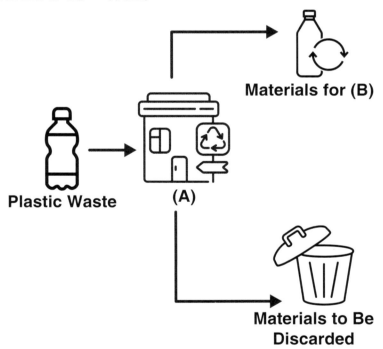

(A) _____

(B) _____

重要字彙

1. **volume** (*n.*) 數量 ③
· Publishing a book requires a considerable **volume** of work that involves different areas of expertise.
出版一本書需要大量作業，其中涉及不同領域的專業。

2. **overwhelm** (*v.*) 使無法承受 ⑤
· During the press conference, the celebrity was **overwhelmed** by the journalists' questions.
在記者會上，該位名人無法承受記者的問題。

3. **capacity** (*n.*) 能力 ④
· AI technology has, in many ways, exceeded human **capacities**.
人工智慧科技已經在許多方面上超越人類的能力。

4. **deposit** (*v.*) 放置 ③
· You can **deposit** this pile of books at the rear of the office for the time being.
你可以將這堆書暫時放置於辦公室後面。

5. **contents** (*n.*) 內容物 ④
· The police examine the **contents** of the bag to see if there are any drugs.
警方檢視袋子裡的內容物以確認是否有毒品。

6. **contract** (*n.*) 契約 ②
· Remember to carefully read through a **contract** before you sign it.
記得在你簽約前先仔細讀過合約。

7. **award** (*v.*) 給予 ③
· All the employees were **awarded** a pay raise for their hard work in such a difficult time.
所有員工因他們在如此艱困時期的辛勞而獲得加薪。

8. **financial** (*adj.*) 經濟的 ④
· During the pandemic lockdowns, a lot of families experienced **financial** difficulties.
疫情封鎖期間，許多家庭經歷了經濟困難。

9. **discard** (*v.*) 丟棄 ⑥

· When **discarding** medical waste, one should follow a strict procedure to avoid contamination.

丟棄醫療廢棄物的時候，應遵照嚴謹的程序以免發生汙染。

10. **toss** (*v.*) 扔 ③

· Don't **toss** your phone around like that. It is not a toy, and you can't afford to break it.

不要這樣扔你的手機。它不是玩具，摔壞了你可無法負擔。

11. **scoop** (*v.*) 鏟起 ④

· Simon kept **scooping** ice cream into his bowl, and emptied half of the bucket within minutes.

Simon 一直將冰淇淋鏟進他的碗裡，不到幾分鐘他就挖空了半桶。

12. **compact** (*v.*) 壓緊 ⑤

· Leo **compacts** the snow to make snowballs and throws them at his playmates.

Leo 將雪壓緊做成雪球，然後丟向他的玩伴。

13. **beam** (*n.*) 光束 ③

· Godzilla shot a laser **beam** from its mouth, destroying the war planes that attacked it.

哥吉拉從口中射出雷射光，擊毀了攻擊牠的戰機。

14. **grind** (*v.*) 磨 (碎) ④

· Some people prefer **grinding** their own coffee beans; they believe it makes their coffee taste better.

有些人喜歡自己磨咖啡豆；他們認為這樣讓他們的咖啡更好喝。

15. **flake** (*n.*) 小薄片 ⑥

· Judy spread some chocolate **flakes** on the top of the cake she just finished making.

Judy 灑一些巧克力小薄片在她剛做好的蛋糕上。

16. **fabric** (*n.*) 布料 ⑤

· The wedding dress is made of a **fabric** that is beautiful to look at but very uncomfortable to wear.

這件婚紗由一種看起來很美麗但穿起來很不舒服的布料做成。

◯─◯ 參考字彙

1. recovery facility (*n.*) 資源回收設施
2. conveyer belt (*n.*) 輸送帶
3. detector (*n.*) 偵測器
4. loader (*n.*) 裝貨機

Note

....

....

....

....

....

....

....

....

....

....

....

....

....

....

Unit 11

Is It Going Too Far When Robots Are Programmed to Kill?

Warm-up Questions

1. Have you seen any robots in your daily life?

2. What are some of the applications of robots?

3. Can you name any works in pop culture regarding killer robots?

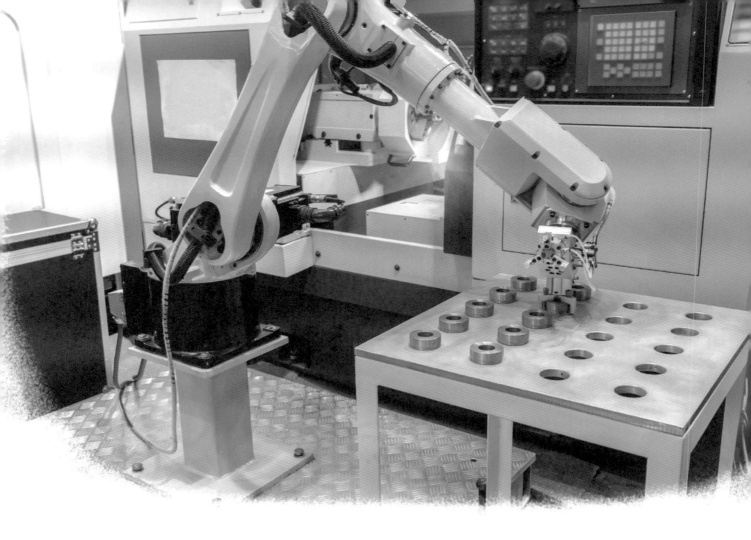

Technology has changed the world dramatically. Among the most striking developments are machines—robots—that can do many things people had to do themselves in the past. Mechanical robots were first developed in the early 20th century, and the earliest electronic ones emerged in the 1940s.

Robots are widely used in various industries to do work that is too boring—usually because it is repetitive and requires no special skills—or too dangerous for human workers. One example is assembly line work in factories that involves performing the same motions over and over again, like putting automobiles together. Humans find it tiresome, but robots won't ever complain, don't get sick or injured, and never need to rest.

Whereas humans must be paid for their time, once robots have been purchased, the only additional cost is regular maintenance. This saves companies money in the long run.

Robots are also capable of doing work that requires a high degree of precision beyond what human hands and eyes can deliver. Some high-tech applications, like manufacturing computer chips or circuit boards, require such fine motor control. Moreover, unlike humans, robots rarely make mistakes. Robots can go places people can't, like environments without oxygen. They can withstand extremes of temperature that would kill humans, such as operating outdoors in the Arctic environment or near the craters of erupting volcanoes, for example.

For these reasons, robots are increasingly being used by police forces and militaries to dispose of bombs and enter structures where criminals or enemies are hiding. Weapon systems can be built into them. Robots have even been used to kill armed suspects who were threatening police or other civilians. However, some people strongly object to this. They claim it goes too far and opens the door to a dark future where people must live in constant fear of being killed by machines. What if some programmer makes evil choices, and the robots execute evil actions? Or worse, what if robots become self-aware and decide to turn against humans? If we're not careful about this, there is no saying that killer robots won't become a reality someday.

1. What does "**such fine motor control**" in the third paragraph refer to? (簡答)

_____

2. 請根據選文內容，從第二、三段各選出一個單詞 (word)，分別填入下列兩句的空格，並視語法需要作適當的字形變化，使句子語意完整、語法正確，且符合文意。(填空)

Robots can perform tasks that require no special skills and a great deal of (A) _____, such as assembly line production, which involves the same actions being done again and again.

From making computer chips with precision to operating in dangerous environments and under (B) _____ temperatures, robots in many ways exceed human capabilities.

_____ 3. According to the passage, which of the following best describes the author's attitude toward the future development of robots? (單選)

(A) Frustrated.   (B) Optimistic.   (C) Objective.   (D) Worried.

_____ 4. According to the passage, which of the following applications of robots is faced with objections? (單選)

(A)

(B)

(C)

(D)

重要字彙

1. **dramatically** (*adv.*) 顯著地
· Discussions on the topic of national security have **dramatically** increased in recent years.
關於國家安全主題的討論在近幾年已顯著地增加。

2. **striking** (*adj.*) 驚人的 ⑤
· It is **striking** how the buildings of this town have remained unchanged for over a century.
這座城鎮的建築能超過一個世紀維持不變相當驚人。

3. **mechanical** (*adj.*) 機械的 ④
· A **mechanical** watch is a watch driven by springs that have to be wound regularly.
機械錶是一種由發條驅動且需要定期上弦的錶。

4. **industry** (*n.*) 產業 ②
· Government officials will provide financial aid to **industries** affected by the pandemic.
政府官員將提供經濟援助給受疫情影響的產業。

5. **repetitive** (*adj.*) 重複的
· Bob is bored of doing **repetitive** tasks every day at work.
Bob 對每天上班做著重複的工作感到無聊。

6. **tiresome** (*adj.*) 令人厭倦的 ⑥
· Lately, Peter has found his job more and more **tiresome** and begun to think of quitting.
最近，Peter 覺得自己的工作越來越令人厭倦，於是開始萌生辭職的念頭。

7. **maintenance** (*n.*) 維修 ⑤
· Heavy machinery needs to shut down for **maintenance** once a year.
重型機具需要每年一次關機維修。

8. **precision** (*n.*) 精確性 ⑥
· Many ancient civilizations had already developed methods to measure the land with **precision**.
許多古文明已經發展出精確丈量土地的方法。

9. **application** (*n.*) 應用 ④
· GIS has many **applications** in terms of analyzing geographical phenomena.
地理資訊系統就分析地理現象的層面上能有很多應用。

10. **chip** (*n.*) (電腦) 晶片 ③

· Semiconductor **chips** are now considered valuable strategic resources by many countries.

半導體晶片如今被許多國家視為重要的戰略物資。

11. **withstand** (*v.*) 承受

· Fighter pilots are trained to **withstand** enormous G-force while flying.

戰鬥機飛行員被訓練在飛行時能承受巨大的 G 力。

12. **crater** (*n.*) 火山口 ⑥

· Over millions of years, the **crater** of the extinct volcano has become a lake.

經過數百萬年後,這座死火山的火山口變成了一座湖。

13. **erupt** (*v.*) (火山) 爆發 ⑤

· Even if the volcanoes in Yangmingshan National Park are likely to **erupt**, it will be in the distant future.

即便陽明山國家公園的火山可能爆發,那也是很久以後的事。

14. **suspect** (*n.*) 嫌犯 ③

· The police exchanged fire on the street with the armed **suspects** that just robbed the bank.

警方與剛搶劫銀行的武裝嫌犯在街上交火。

15. **civilian** (*n.*) 平民 ④

· Soldiers dress as **civilians** in disguise to travel through war zones undetected.

士兵們喬裝成平民以便穿過戰區而不被發現。

16. **self-aware** (*adj.*) 有自我意識的

· AI that becomes **self-aware** and destructive to humans is the premise of many sci-fi movies.

人工智慧變得有自我意識且對人類產生危害是許多科幻電影的背景。

○─○ 參考字彙

1. assembly line (*n.*) 裝配線
2. circuit board (*n.*) 電路板
3. Arctic (*adj.*) 北極的

Note

Unit 12

Twinkle, Twinkle—
Could There Be Diamonds
in Space?

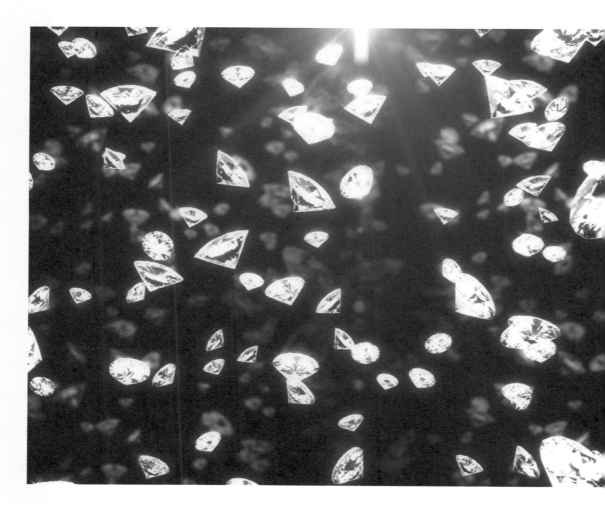

Warm-up Questions

1. How are diamonds formed on Earth?

2. What are the characteristics of Saturn and Jupiter?

3. Why might there be diamonds on Saturn and Jupiter?

They sparkle and quite literally cost a fortune. They are diamonds—formed when carbon deep below the surface of the Earth is subject to high heat plus extreme pressure. Over billions of years, super-heated carbon is gradually transformed under the crushing weight of the Earth's crust. Diamonds are the end product of this long and slow process. Of course, seen from another way, that's just the beginning. Diamonds must be mined from the ground using heavy equipment, cut using special tools and techniques, and highly polished before they end up on engagement rings, necklaces, crowns, and other jewelry.

Scientists think these gems, which have captured the human imagination for centuries, might exist in great quantities on other planets in our solar system, too. Specifically, researchers point to Saturn and Jupiter—the two planets known as gas giants. Neither is solid; both are actually dense balls of gas with, presumably, solid cores. Although conditions are much different from what we find on Earth, the key ingredients for forming diamonds—heat and pressure—are both present.

What's more, as their name suggests, the gas giants are massive. Picture it this way: seven hundred and sixty-four Earth-sized planets could fit inside Saturn, while a thousand three hundred and twenty-one of them could be squeezed inside Jupiter. But without the weight of a hard outer crust to create pressure, how could these gas giant planets ever produce diamonds?

Using what they know about the composition of Saturn and Jupiter, scientists have created models to answer this question. They believe the planets' strong gravity and high temperatures could form diamonds from a certain compound, methane, suspended in mid-air. It could work like this: when methane is struck by lightning, the heat turns it into tiny bits of carbon. As the carbon sinks down into the deeper layers of the planets, the intense pressure and high heat could turn it into diamonds. Scientists use the image of "diamond rain" to explain how this amazing phenomenon might look.

1. 請根據選文內容，從第一段及第四段中各選出一個單詞 (word)，分別填入下列兩句的空格，並視語法需要作適當的字形變化，使句子語意完整、語法正確，且符合文意。(填空)

When carbon deep within the Earth is subject to high temperature and pressure, diamond (A) _____ occurs.

When methane is (B) _____ with the heat of lightning, it can turn into carbon, which is the raw material for diamonds.

2. What does "**these gems**" in the second paragraph refer to? (簡答)

_____

_____ 3. 請從下列 (A) 到 (F) 中，選出文章對 diamond rain 敘述正確的選項。
(多選題)

(A) Scientists have been planning to mine diamonds on Saturn and Jupiter.

(B) Diamond rain begins in mid-air, where lightning turns methane into carbon.

(C) Diamonds are found in the deep layers of Saturn and Jupiter by scientists.

(D) Saturn and Jupiter produce diamonds because they have a hard outer crust.

(E) It is possible to produce diamond rain on Earth with more research done.

(F) On Saturn and Jupiter, enormous amounts of pressure and heat could turn carbon into diamonds.

重要字彙

1. **sparkle** (*v.*) 閃耀 ⑤
 · Klara's large diamond ring **sparkles** every time she moves her hand.
   Klara 的大鑽戒在她每次移動她的手時就會跟著閃耀。

2. **literally** (*adv.*) 實在地
 · Hamish **literally** doesn't care how people perceive him at all.
   Hamish 實在完全不在乎人們怎麼看他。

3. **carbon** (*n.*) 碳 ⑤
 · **Carbon** emissions produced by human activity have affected the global climate.
   人類活動製造的碳排放影響了全球氣候。

4. **crushing** (*adj.*) 重壓的
 · I am under the **crushing** pressure of trying to finish three projects due on the same day.
   我正承受試圖在同一天完成三個到期計劃的沉重壓力。

5. **mine** (*v.*) 開採 (礦) ①
 · In the movie *Avatar*, people from Earth invade a planet called Pandora to **mine** a precious mineral that is only found there.
   在電影《阿凡達》裡，來自地球的人入侵名叫潘朵拉的星球，以開採一種只有在那裡才找得到的珍貴礦物。

6. **polish** (*v.*) 磨光 ④
 · It's important to know how to **polish** shoes to keep them looking shiny and new.
   知道如何為鞋子磨光以使它們看起來又亮又新是重要的。

7. **capture** (*v.*) 引發 ③
 · Cate's paintings **capture** an art dealer's attention, and he wants to put them on auction.
   Cate 的畫作引起了一名藝術經銷商的注意，他想要將它們拿去拍賣。

8. **solid** (*adj.*) 固體的 ③
 · During Jim's recovery, he could not have any **solid** food; he could only consume fluids.
   在 Jim 的康復期間，他不能吃固體食物；他只能攝取流質。

9. **dense** (*adj.*) 厚重的 ④

· A **dense** fog suddenly hit the town and caused many traffic accidents because people couldn't see where they were driving.

一陣濃霧突然侵襲了這座城鎮並造成許多交通事故，因為人們無法辨識他們行駛的方向。

10. **presumably** (*adv.*) 據推測 ⑤

· The suspect, **presumably**, traveled on foot after he ditched his vehicle.

據推測，這名嫌犯在拋棄他的車後以步行的方式移動。

11. **massive** (*adj.*) 巨大的 ⑤

· When the rocket launched into the sky, it created a **massive** blast that stunned the viewers.

當火箭升空時，它產生了巨大衝擊聲，震驚了觀看者。

12. **squeeze** (*v.*) 擠壓 ③

· I never like large gatherings because you have to **squeeze** through the crowd if you wish to move.

我從來不喜歡大型聚會，因為如果你想要移動，你就得擠過人群。

13. **composition** (*n.*) 成分 ④

· Coal and diamonds are similar in chemical **composition**.

煤炭和鑽石在化學成分上相似。

14. **gravity** (*n.*) 重力 ⑤

· When you parachute, just remember your training, and let **gravity** do the rest.

當你跳傘的時候，只需記住你的訓練，並讓重力完成剩下的事。

15. **compound** (*n.*) 化合物 ⑤

· Water is a **compound** of oxygen and hydrogen.

水是氧和氫的化合物。

16. **suspend** (*v.*) 懸浮 ⑤

· The artist **suspended** her work from the ceiling using strings and wires for display.

藝術家以線絲將她的作品懸浮於天花板來作展示。

👓 參考字彙

1. Saturn (*n.*) 土星
2. Jupiter (*n.*) 木星
3. methane (*n.*) 甲烷

慣用語和片語

1. **be subject to** 受…影響
· All trains **are subject to** delay caused by the earthquake.
　所有列車皆因地震而受到延誤。

Note

Unit 13

Ocean Pollution Victims

Warm-up Questions

1. Why are the lives of marine animals threatened?

2. How do plastics in the ocean affect marine life?

3. How do rising water temperatures impact whales?

Marine pollution directly impacts marine life. Some of the common victims include sea turtles, coral reefs, sharks, seabirds, and whales.

 Sea turtles breed slowly, which means their population grows slowly. Therefore, they are more vulnerable to ecological threats. Sea turtles mistake plastic bags for food, resulting in health issues and death due to plastic intake.

 Coral reefs are highly complex and delicate systems made up of millions of individual species. They are easily affected by changes and disruptions in the environment like rising water temperatures, ocean acidification, and plastic waste that is thrown into the ocean.

Besides environmental pollution, sharks also face the threat from fishing activities. Entanglement in nets or fishing lines always endangers the lives of sharks. It's common to see a shark with a hook in its jaws or fishing lines around its body as it swims away.

Seabirds, such as gulls and pelicans, often mistake plastics for fish or insects. They eat these items or become entangled in them, which can lead to injury or death. Oil spills can also be a disaster for seabirds. The oil covers their feathers and disables them from flying.

Whales, the largest mammals on Earth, are also affected by marine pollution. Rising water temperatures causes the organisms which whales feed on to change their habitats. This means whales have to spend more time locating their food source, leaving them less time to reproduce.

_____ 1. Which marine animals need to migrate longer and farther to survive? (單選)

(A) Sea turtles.　　(B) Sharks.　　　(C) Seabirds.　　　(D) Whales.

2. Which word in the passage means "the act of taking something into one's body"? (簡答)

_____

3–5. What are the possible dangers that each kind of the creatures faces? From (A) to (F) below, fill in the blanks based on the information in the passage. (單選)

(A)　　　　　　　　　(B)　　　　　　　　　(C)

(D)　　　　　　　　　(E)　　　　　　　　　(F)

Creatures	Possible Dangers
Sea Turtles	A
Coral Reefs	A, ___3___
Sharks	___4___
Seabirds	A, ___5___
Whales	C

3. _____　4. _____　5. _____

96

重要字彙

1. **marine** (*adj.*) 海洋的 ⑤
· If humans do not regulate fishing activity, **marine** resources will soon be drained.
如果人類不去管制漁業活動，海洋資源將會很快枯竭。

2. **impact** (*v.*) 衝擊 ④
· The COVID-19 pandemic heavily **impacted** our ways of living and our state of mind.
COVID-19 疫情重重地衝擊我們的生活方式和心理狀態。

3. **victim** (*n.*) 受害者 ③
· **Victims** of climate change hazards are often the ones who contribute the least to climate change.
氣候變遷災害的受害者往往是對氣候變遷的影響程度最小的人。

4. **breed** (*v.*) 繁殖 ④
· Household pests are difficult to eliminate because they **breed** like a disease.
居家害蟲難以消滅，因為牠們像疫病一樣繁殖。

5. **vulnerable** (*adj.*) 易受⋯傷害的 ⑤
· Old paintings are **vulnerable** to changes in temperature and humidity.
舊畫容易因溫度和濕度的變化而受損。

6. **ecological** (*adj.*) 生態的 ⑤
· Activists argue that the construction of the highway bridge will be an **ecological** disaster to the region.
激進分子主張這座公路橋的建造將會成為這個地區的生態浩劫。

7. **intake** (*n.*) 攝入 ⑥
· To stay healthy, you should maintain a balanced **intake** of food.
要保持健康，你應該維持均衡的食物攝取。

8. **delicate** (*adj.*) 嬌弱的 ④
· Mice that are bred as pets are very **delicate**. They cannot survive in the wild.
被培育為寵物的老鼠非常嬌弱。牠們無法於野外生存。

9. **disruption** (*n.*) 干擾
· Heavy snow has caused major **disruptions** to traffic in the northern part of the country.
大雪對該國北部的交通造成重大干擾。

disrupt (*v.*) 干擾 ⑤

· Our conversation is **disrupted** by the noises that surround us.
我們的對話被我們周圍的噪音所干擾。

10. **hook** (*n.*) 釣魚鉤 ④

· To prevent your **hook** from hurting anyone, be careful to cast your fishing rod correctly.
為避免你的釣魚鉤傷到人，要小心並正確地拋你的魚竿。

11. **jaw** (*n.*) 下頜 ③

· Amanda's **jaw** dropped when she learned that her favorite band will play live in her hometown.
Amanda 聽到她最愛的樂團要到她的家鄉作現場演出時，她的下巴都掉下來了。

12. **disable** (*v.*) 使失去能力 ⑥

· Most of the planes were **disabled** by the air strike before they had a chance to take off.
大多數的飛機在來得及升空之前就被空襲所癱瘓了。

13. **mammal** (*n.*) 哺乳類動物 ⑤

· Hawks are a kind of predator birds that feed on small **mammals** such as rabbits.
鷹為一種猛禽，以像是兔子等小型哺乳動物為食。

14. **organism** (*n.*) 生物 ⑤

· Every **organism** has the instinct of self-preservation that drives it to stay away from harm.
每一種生物都具有自我保存的本能，驅使牠們遠離危害。

15. **habitat** (*n.*) 棲息地 ⑤

· The government plans to establish a natural reserve to conserve the **habitat** of black bears.
政府計劃建立一座自然保護區以保育黑熊的棲地。

16. **reproduce** (*v.*) 繁殖 ⑥

· Salmon return to the places they were born to **reproduce**.
鮭魚會回到牠們的出生地來繁殖。

○─○ 參考字彙

1. coral reef (*n.*) 珊瑚礁
2. acidification (*n.*) 酸化
3. entanglement (*n.*) 纏住
4. oil spill (*n.*) 漏油

Note

Unit 14

Pride of Taiwan

Warm-up Questions

1. What did An-ting do to promote rural education?

2. Why did Bo-wei decide to return to Taiwan?

3. Who else do you think are the Pride of Taiwan?

"Pride of Taiwan" was first mentioned in newspaper reports in 2001. The title used to refer to the Taiwanese who won in international competitions, but it now refers to the ones that attract international attention for their achievements. Here are two young Prides of Taiwan and their stories.

An-ting Liu, born in 1989, is the founder of Teach for Taiwan. An-ting's involvement in education for underprivileged groups began in her college years. While studying in Princeton University, she spent a lot of time working in different countries, such as Haiti, Cambodia, France, and Switzerland. Eventually, she gained her bachelor's degree in Public and International Affairs with flying colors. However, she couldn't stop thinking about what she could do to help her home country.

Inspired by her college friend, Wendy Kopp, the founder of "Teach for America," An-ting started to collaborate with organizations in Taiwan on the issues of rural education upon graduating from university. In 2014, An-ting returned home and founded Teach for Taiwan (TFT). Through TFT, she has recruited young graduates from Taiwanese universities to teach in remote public schools.

An-ting strives to make a contribution to rural education and help children with fewer resources by creating an equal and high-quality educational environment. In 2016, she was selected by *Forbes* magazine as one of the thirty most influential people under thirty in Asia.

Bo-wei Yang, born in 1990, is the head chef of Sinasera 24 in Taitung. At age 23, Bo-wei won the championship in a European food carving tournament. Having worked as a chef in a Three MICHELIN Star restaurant in Marseille, France for years, he decided to go back to Taiwan and opened a restaurant that would feature local cultures and embody his personality.

Bo-wei's grandmother was a cook and his mother was a food vendor, so he had inherited foodie genes ever since he was little. In his childhood, he often watched a Japanese gourmet show and was amazed at each delicate dish. It was that period of time that led Bo-wei to pursue his chef dream. Years later, when Bo-wei was working in France, he was approached by a guesthouse owner from Taitung and was presented with the opportunity to become the head chef of his restaurant. Bo-wei accepted the invitation and returned to Taiwan.

Unlike other young chefs whose sole and ultimate goal is to win MICHELIN Stars, Bo-wei is more obsessed with discovering local ingredients and puts effort into experimenting with them. "What I want to convey is the taste of the ingredients themselves, not piles of techniques." Bo-wei said.

1. 請根據選文內容，從兩則故事中各選出一個單詞 (word)，分別填入下列兩句的空格，並視語法需要作適當的字形變化，使句子語意完整、語法正確，且符合全文文意。(填空)

   With her passion and love for Taiwan, An-ting Liu is willing to (A) _____ to education in order to help children in rural areas.

   Bo-wei Yang returned to Taitung in (B) _____ of his dream of opening a restaurant that features local ingredients.

2. Which word in An-ting Liu's story means "to work with someone in order to achieve a certain purpose"? (簡答)

   _____

_____ 3. 請從下列 (A) 到 (F) 中，選出對 An-ting Liu 和 Bo-wei Yang 都正確的選項。(多選題)

   (A) Growing up in rural areas of Taiwan.

   (B) Receiving education in foreign countries.

   (C) Showing outstanding achievements in their fields.

   (D) Winning awards in several international competitions.

   (E) Returning to their home country to realize their dreams.

   (F) Gaining fame through sacrificing themselves for Taiwan.

重要字彙

1. **achievement** (*n.*) 成就 ③
   · Vicky considers her greatest **achievement** to be finding new homes for over ten stray animals.
   Vicky 認為她最大的成就是為超過十隻流浪動物找到新家。

2. **founder** (*n.*) 創辦人 ④
   · Being the son of the company's **founder**, Olson will take over the business when the time comes.
   Olson 身為公司創辦人的兒子，會於時機成熟的時候接手事業。

3. **involvement** (*n.*) 參與 ④
   · Eileen's **involvement** in the project proves to be a great help.
   Eileen 對這項計劃的參與經證明有莫大的幫助。

4. **underprivileged** (*adj.*) 弱勢的
   · **Underprivileged** children need additional care during winter and summer vacation.
   弱勢兒童在寒暑假期間需要特別關照。

   privilege (*n.*) 特權 ④
   · A man of **privilege** such as you can never understand what it means to be completely poor.
   像你這樣的特權人士永遠無法了解徹底窮困的感覺。

5. **bachelor** (*n.*) 學士 ⑥
   · Schmidt has a **bachelor's** degree in geography from National Taiwan Normal University.
   Schmidt 擁有國立臺灣師範大學地理學的學士學位。

6. **inspire** (*v.*) 啟發 ④
   · The story of the Taiwanese director Ang Lee **inspires** Janet to pursue a career in the movie business.
   臺灣導演李安的故事啟發 Janet 進入電影產業追求志業。

7. **collaborate** (*v.*) 合作
   · Woody **collaborates** with Buzz on designing and making toys.
   Woody 與 Buzz 合作設計與製造玩具。

collaboration (*n.*) 合作 ⑤

· Urban planning requires the **collaboration** between the government and its citizens.
都市計劃需要政府與市民的合作。

8. **recruit** (*v.*) 徵召 ⑤

· The army has been **recruiting** civilians to defend the city.
軍隊在徵召平民來防衛城市。

9. **remote** (*adj.*) 偏遠的 ③

· Darren often travels to **remote** parts of the country to study the ecologies there.
Darren 經常旅行至國內偏遠地區以研究那邊的生態。

10. **contribution** (*n.*) 貢獻 ④

· I'm glad I am able to make a small **contribution** to the preservation of railway cultures.
我很榮幸自己能夠對鐵道文化的保存作出微小的貢獻。

11. **influential** (*adj.*) 有影響力的 ④

· Paul is highly **influential** in deciding which project should be promoted first.
Paul 對於哪個計劃應該先被推動具有高度影響力。

12. **championship** (*n.*) 冠軍 ④

· Lee Yang and Wang Chi-lin won the badminton **championship** at the Tokyo Olympics.
李洋和王齊麟贏得了東京奧運的羽球冠軍。

13. **tournament** (*n.*) 錦標賽 ⑤

· International football **tournaments** such as the FIFA World Cup often draw a lot of attention.
像國際足球總會世界盃這樣的國際足球錦標賽往往吸引很多目光。

14. **embody** (*v.*) 體現

· People in this country **embody** the spirit of resistance in the darkest of times.
該國的人民在最黑暗的時刻體現了反抗的精神。

15. **inherit** (*v.*) 遺傳 ⑤

· Carl **inherits** his mother's hospitality and always greets people around him cheerfully.
Carl 遺傳了他媽媽好客的性情，總是會開朗地向週遭的人打招呼。

16. **approach** (*v.*) 聯繫 ②

· Scarlett was **approached** by an agent and asked if she was interested in modeling.

  Scarlett 被一位經紀人聯繫，並問她是否有意願當模特兒。

17. **sole** (*adj.*) 唯一的 ⑥

· When Ryan woke up in the hospital, the staff told him that he was the **sole** survivor of the accident.

  當 Ryan 在醫院醒來的時候，醫務人員跟他說他是這場意外唯一的生還者。

18. **ultimate** (*adj.*) 最終的 ⑤

· The ruler's **ultimate** goal is to secure his regime permanently.

  這名統治者最終的目標是永久確立他的政權。

19. **obsess** (*v.*) 執著 ⑥

· Elena is still **obsessed** with Saul even though they broke up months ago.

  Elena 仍對 Saul 感到執著，即便他們好幾個月前就分手了。

◯◯ 參考字彙

1. gourmet (*n.*) 美食家

Note

英文素養寫作攻略

郭慧敏 編著

將寫作理論具象化,打造一套好理解的寫作方法!

本書特色

1. 了解大考英文作文素養命題重點,掌握正確審題、構思與布局要領。

2. 從認識文體、寫作思考串聯到掌握關鍵句型,逐步練好寫作基本功。

3. 提供大考各類寫作題型技巧剖析與範文佳句,全面提升英文寫作力。

神拿滿級分——英文學測總複習(二版)

孫至娟　編著

- 重點搭配練習：雙效合一有感複習，讓你應試力 UP！

- 議題式心智圖：補充時事議題單字，讓你單字力 UP！

- 文章主題多元：符合學測多元取材，讓你閱讀力 UP！

- 混合題最素養：多樣混合題型訓練，讓你理解力 UP！

- 獨立作文頁面：作答空間超好運用，讓你寫作力 UP！

- 詳盡解析考點：見題拆題精闢解析，讓你解題力 UP！

新多益
黃金互動16週：

基礎篇／進階篇（二版）

李海碩、張秀帆、多益900團隊 編著

依難易度分為基礎篇與進階篇，教師可依學生程度選用。

- ★ 本書由ETS認證多益英語測驗專業發展工作坊講師李海碩、張秀帆編寫，及多益模擬試題編寫者Joseph E. Schier審訂。
- ★ 涵蓋2018年3月最新改制多益題型。每冊各8單元皆附電子朗讀音檔及一份多益全真模擬試題。

國家圖書館出版品預行編目資料

學測英文混合題實戰演練／溫宥基編著.——初版一
刷.——臺北市：三民，2023
面；　公分.——(英語Make Me High系列)

ISBN 978-957-14-7621-6　（平裝）
1. 英語教學 2. 讀本 3. 中等教育

524.38　　　　　　　　　　　　　112003030

英語 Make Me High 系列

學測英文混合題實戰演練

| 編 著 者 | 溫宥基 |
| 責任編輯 | 施牧之 |

發 行 人	劉振強
出 版 者	三民書局股份有限公司
地　　址	臺北市復興北路 386 號 (復北門市)
	臺北市重慶南路一段 61 號 (重南門市)
電　　話	(02)25006600
網　　址	三民網路書店 https://www.sanmin.com.tw

出版日期	初版一刷 2023 年 4 月
書籍編號	S872400
Ｉ Ｓ Ｂ Ｎ	978-957-14-7621-6

三民書局

108 課綱適用

英語 *Make Me High* 系列

學測英文
混合題實戰演練

解析本

溫宥基 編著

三民書局

CONTENTS

Unit 3

1. A 2. D 3. AD 4. entertained

現代歌曲和舞蹈的非洲文化根源

　　十六世紀期間，許多非洲人被強行帶走、裝載上船，被帶到北美及南美工作成為奴工。他們被迫工作又領不到錢，常被主人惡劣地毆打並懲罰。

　　舞蹈一直以來是這些非洲人文化的一部分。雖然被賣掉當奴隸剝奪了他們的自由與人權，但卻不能抹去他們對文化傳統和家鄉的記憶。在避開主人的視線時，這些非洲人持續跳舞，儘管這不被允許。為了避免被抓到破壞規矩，他們跳舞時不會抬起腳，取而代之的是在地面上拖曳著雙腳。同時，他們會移動臀部，擺動著上身。他們工作時也會唱歌。跳舞和唱歌幫助他們些許地減輕日常生活的苦楚。

　　到了十九世紀，白人注意到這些奴隸的舞蹈及歌唱能力，開始上臺模仿他們來娛樂白人觀眾。這些表演稱為「黑人劇團 (minstrel shows)」。隨著表演的人氣漸長，白人對這些非洲人才能的欽羨之意也隨之高漲。1920年代及 1930 年代出現的幾種受歡迎的舞蹈類型，正是由白人模仿非洲人的舞步而來的。這些包括了吉特巴舞以及查理斯頓舞。這段期間也見證了踢踏舞的誕生，它融合了非洲人及愛爾蘭新移民的舞蹈。

　　從那時起，非洲人透過歌曲及舞蹈，持續影響西方的流行文化。爵士、藍調音樂以及嘻哈，都有非裔美人的根源。再者，現代的街舞類型，像是霹靂舞、鎖舞和機械舞，都是由非裔美人發明並改良的。的確，我們可以合理地說，沒有非洲人的貢獻，我們所知的現代音樂及舞蹈是不會存在的，至少以西方世界來說確實如此。

1. 本題評量學生能否理解文章大意，掌握文章主旨。本文主旨在解說現代音樂與舞蹈的來源與發展。作答線索在一、三、四段的開頭，三者都有時間或時序推移的敘述，以鋪陳現代歌曲及舞蹈從非洲文化發展的先後順序，故正解為 (A)「解釋現代歌曲與舞蹈的發展。」
(B)「倡導現代歌曲與舞蹈的優勢。」、(C)「檢視現代歌曲與舞蹈的特色。」、(D)「提倡現代歌曲與舞蹈的文化價值」皆非正解。

2. 本題評量學生能否在閱讀文章後，掌握文章架構，進行歸納與統整，理解文章陳述現代歌曲及舞蹈從非洲文化發展的先後順序。本文按時間順序 (chronological order) 敘述現代歌曲及舞蹈的發展，依序分別為 b. African slavery「非洲奴隸制度」，c. Africans' dancing and singing while laboring「非洲人勞動時跳舞唱歌」，d. white people's copying「白人模仿」，最後是 a. African Americans' continuing influence「非裔美人持續的影響」。如此才會在今日美國的流行音樂及舞蹈中看到非洲的影響，故 (D) 為正解。

3. 本題評量學生能否掌握文章發展與細節。

(A)「舞蹈及歌唱有助舒緩非洲人身為奴隸的艱苦生活。」答案線索在第二段最後一句；(D)「白人模仿學習非洲人的舞步，也對現代舞蹈有所貢獻。」答案線索在第三段第四句。故 (A) 和 (D) 為正解。

(B)「現代音樂與舞蹈與非洲人和他們的貢獻不大有關聯。」根據文意，現代音樂與舞蹈起源於非洲人及歸功於他們的貢獻；(C)「許多非洲人被帶到南北美洲為了白人做表演而用。」根據文意，非洲人被帶到南北美洲是因為奴隸制度的關係；(E)「奴隸制度奪走非洲人的自由、人權以及他們的唱歌和跳舞的能力。」根據文意，非洲人雖被迫成為奴隸，但在勞動時仍持續唱歌跳舞來紓解壓力；(F)「西方流行文化幾乎沒有和非洲文化混和，造就現今的音樂與舞蹈。」根據文意，西方流行文化與非洲文化大有相關，也造就現今的流行音樂與舞蹈。故 (B)、(C)、(E) 和 (F) 皆非正解。

4. 本題評量學生能否依據上下文脈絡，從指定的段落中選出一個單詞，並運用語意及語法的知識，做適當字形變化，寫出正解。空格的句子陳述「黑人劇團在十九世紀受到極度歡迎，表演者在劇中藉由模仿黑人來**娛樂**白人。」根據文意，可以選擇第三段第一句的動詞 entertain (娛樂)，變化成過去式動詞 entertained，故正解為 entertained。

Unit 4

1. BF　2. convention/Convention.
3. ❶　4. D

無聊電視節目的神奇吸引力

隨著科技快速發展，生活的步調也持續加速。我們常常被我們的電子裝置、最愛的應用程式以及網際網路佔據，這甚至暗示著人們較難專注在需要花費較長時間的事物上。我們要多變性。我們要娛樂。我們要新穎、多采多姿且因此刺激的事物。而且，我們現在就要！

❶當我們似乎變得較往日更沒耐性時，人們卻轉而朝著某個較慢步調的方向尋找娛樂，這在現下的時代也許顯得奇特。❷然而一個新的現象稱為「慢電視」正席捲世界風潮。❸這個概念來自挪威。❹這種新型態電視節目的製作人，可以說是決定把老舊的規則手冊拋出窗外。❺他們摒棄傳統，例如言談對話、姣好面貌的演員班底，以及堆砌刺激高潮的故事情節。❻同時，他們決定要繼續秉持著「實境電視」的理念 —— 這在近年來已被證明是一套受到歡迎的電視型態。

最終產出的節目以人們連續好幾個小時從事著日常活動為特色。想想看十四個小時不間斷地賞鳥，或是連續十八小時的釣魚活動。不符合你的速度？那麼十二小時搭船旅行，或是七小時搭火車遊歷下雪的挪威鄉村呢？

這些製作人選擇了一種不同說故

事的方式，讓觀眾自行編造故事。觀眾看到的是他們可以輕易認同理解的畫面，深植於他們的文化中，並被帶入一趟讓他們身歷其境的旅程。當觀眾開始注意到小細節，很自然會促使他們去問問題。因為觀眾只能和自己互動，他們必須自行編造故事以滿足好奇心，進而引發他們的想像力。

1. 本題評量學生能否掌握文章細節。(B)「慢電視鼓勵人們發揮他們的想像力。」答案線索在最後一段最後一句；(F)「慢電視結合實境電視概念和日常活動。」答案線索在第二段最後一句及第三段第一句。故 (B) 和 (F) 為正解。

   (A)「慢電視提倡經典電影及默片。」不符文意。第二段和第三段描述慢電視的節目內容，並沒有提到經典電影和默片；(C)「慢電視是以最新且充滿戲劇性情節的電視節目為特色。」不符文意。根據第二段第五句和第三段第一句，慢電視的節目特色是人們連續幾個小時從事著日常活動，沒有高潮迭起或是充滿戲劇性的故事情節；(D)「慢電視呈現俊男美女們的對話。」不符文意。根據第二段第五句，慢電視沒有言談對話，沒有面貌姣好的卡司；(E)「慢電視採用先進科技來提供娛樂。」不符文意。文章並沒有提到前述內容。故 (A)、(C)、(D) 和 (E) 皆非正解。

2. 本題評量學生能否理解文意，並根據題幹說明，從文中選出一個單詞作為答案。題目詢問的是哪一個字詞跟「規則手冊 (rule book)」的字義最接近。第二段第四句指出，慢電視要「把老舊的規則手冊拋出窗外 (throw the old rule book out the window)」，第二段第五句接續指出，這個做法「摒棄傳統 (did away with conventions)」。依據上下文脈絡，運用語意知識，把規則手冊拋出窗外即是摒棄傳統的意思，故正解為 convention。

3. 本題評量學生能否掌握文意，並加以舉證。題目詢問第二段的哪一句話最能顯示作者有意引起讀者對慢電視產生好奇的企圖。第二段第一句指出，當人們變得更沒耐性時，卻尋找比較慢步調的娛樂，在這樣的時代看起來很奇特。此句以 It may seem strange . . . 開頭，即是作者藉由指出慢電視崛起這個奇特的反差，企圖引起讀者對慢電視的好奇心。故正解為❶。

4. 本題評量學生能否掌握文章大意，理解慢電視的播放內容。慢電視播放的內容沒有言談對話或高潮迭起的敘事，而是日常生活的平凡事物，能貼近觀眾的生活並引起共鳴，像是火車旅行等經歷，故 (D) 為正解。(A) 新聞播報；(B) 討論活動；(C) 搖滾演唱會。以上皆非慢電視的節目內容訴求，故非正解。

Unit 5

1. (A) populate; (B) growth/domination
2. C　3. C; 4. F; 5. A; 6. D

森林大火的雙重面貌

森林大火，不論是人類造成的或是因閃電襲擊而引發，通常都被稱為災難。這是有充分理由的：除了樹木以外，森林大火吞噬其路徑中的一切，包括房子與產業。它們可能造成生命及財產的損失，造成悲痛及數百萬元的破壞。撲滅它們極為昂貴而且危險，而且它們所造成的破壞也會持續存在著。房屋可以重建，但是被大火破壞的森林區域一般來說要花上數十年才能再次被樹木覆蓋。當然，原本可以被砍下當作木料的成材樹木遭受毀壞，可認為是經濟上的損失。另一方面，森林的消滅也意味著用來提供戶外旅遊、娛樂及休閒的景點消失了。不論是哪一種，森林是珍貴的天然資源，而森林大火毀壞了它們。

儘管如此，不可否認的是森林大火在大自然中扮演了一個重要的角色。其一，森林大火殺死威脅樹木的昆蟲，例如一種名為光蠟瘦吉丁蟲的甲蟲。沒有大火抑制光蠟瘦吉丁蟲的總數，這個物種會散佈地更遠更快，牠們對光蠟樹的破壞會更廣泛。

再者，森林大火會清理森林上方茂密的樹層，以及覆蓋在森林地面的樹葉和樹枝。一旦這些成材的樹木被消滅，陽光就可以觸及種子及森林地表的幼樹，讓牠們有機會可以生長。

這也讓新的物種，所謂的「先鋒物種」，得以有機會在先前被其他樹種支配的地方立足。

有一件事是確定的，當炎熱乾燥的天氣型態持續，以及人類的城鎮及都市越來越延伸到大自然地區，森林大火將繼續它們的作為，不論好與壞，年復一年。

1. 本題評量學生能否依據上下文脈絡，從指定的段落中各選出一個單詞，並運用語意及語法的知識，作適當的字形變化，寫出正解。
   空格 (A) 的句子陳述「若沒有野火，光蠟瘦吉丁蟲會增生並**棲居於**森林廣大的區域範圍。」根據文意，可以選出第二段第三句的名詞 population (總數)，並依據語法變化成動詞 populate (棲居於)，故空格 (A) 正解為 populate。
   空格 (B) 的句子陳述「野火可以終結成材樹木於一座森林裡的**生長／支配狀態**，並給新樹種生長的空間。」根據文意，可以選出第三段第二句的動詞 grow (生長)，或最後一句的動詞 dominate (支配)，並依據語法變化成名詞 growth (生長) 或 domination (支配狀態)，故空格 (B) 正解為 growth/domination。

2. 本題評量學生能否理解文意，了解 emerald ash borer「光蠟瘦吉丁蟲」對樹木造成的威脅。第二段第二句說明光蠟瘦吉丁蟲是 insects which threaten trees「威脅樹木的昆蟲」，故正解為 (C)「牠們阻礙樹木營養和水分的流動。」

(A)「牠們幫忙清除樹頂茂密的樹層。」、(B)「牠們是樹種研究的好主題。」、(D)「牠們對倚靠樹葉維生的昆蟲造成威脅。」皆不符合文意，故非正解。

3-6. 本題評量學生能否整合及判斷資訊，依照文中森林大火帶來的正面和負面效益進行分類。(A)「森林大火燒毀成材樹木，造成木材損失。」屬於森林大火的負面效益。(B)「森林大火汙染水源，造成動物死亡。」文中並未提及。(C)「森林大火消滅成材樹木，可讓先鋒物種生長。」屬於森林大火的正面效益。(D)「森林大火破壞本來可用來從事休憩活動的森林。」屬於森林大火的負面效益。(E)「森林大火清出林地，讓人類有空間蓋房子。」文中並未提及。(F)「森林大火消滅本來有可能更擴散滋長的昆蟲。」屬於森林大火的正面效益。故正面效益 (good) 為 (C) 和 (F)，負面效益 (bad) 為 (A) 和 (D)。

1. CF　2. compounding/Compounding.
3. (A) avoid putting too much pressure on kids; (B) write down their worries

對數字感到煩惱：數學焦慮的常見問題

　　有一種迷思是男孩的數學比女孩好，但這並非事實。事實是許多男孩和女孩，還有男人和女人，都對數學感到焦慮，並且在必須計算數學時覺得緊張和不自在。

　　想像這個場景：學生坐在教室裡，等著考數學。他們可以感受到自己的心臟在胸口敲擊著。他們的手在發抖，且手掌覆蓋著許多汗。他們擔心自己會失敗，儘管他們已經很努力用功，而且練習解出無數個數學問題。要專心很難，事實上幾乎不可能，而這正是他們要成功通過考試最需要做的事。

　　這聽起來熟悉嗎？如果是的話，你並不孤單。事實上，據估計大約有百分之二十的人罹患像是這樣的症狀，專家稱之為「數學焦慮」。

　　數學焦慮是來自於對失敗的恐懼。這類的自我懷疑經常始於早期的學習經歷。在小學，數學經常在學生面前被描繪成一種本質上具挑戰性且困難的事物。這在年幼的心裡造成了一種預期心態。再者，要學習者做事快一點的壓力也一直存在，像是能記住乘法表或數學公式，而且一被要求就要能背誦。讓問題更加惡化的是，有些文化會把數學能力跟一個人的整體智慧連結在一起。這種觀念讓數學不好

的學生覺得他們有點不夠格。

幸運的是，教育心理學專家很快地向我們保證，數學焦慮是可以克服的。其一，父母和老師們可以試著讓數學較不可怕，並且避免給孩子太多壓力。學生自己也可以嘗試放鬆的技巧，像是深呼吸的練習，以平緩自己的不安。他們也可以將憂慮寫下來，因為這麼做有助於釐清憂慮的實際原因，並且使焦慮變得比較不會那麼難以忍受。

1. 本題評量學生能否整合文章提供的資訊。(C)「辨識數學焦慮的症狀。」文章第二段的內容指出數學焦慮的外顯行為；(F)「提供減輕數學學習擔憂的建議。」文章最後一段提出克服數學焦慮的幾個方法。故 (C) 和 (F) 為正解。

   (A)「設計一份衡量數學能力的測驗。」文章沒有提到設計數學測驗；(B)「將數學技能應用於實際生活情境。」文章主要探討數學的學習狀況，並非談論數學應用情境；(D)「執行一個估算數學焦慮的調查。」文章提出克服數學焦慮的方法，而不是估算數學焦慮的調查；(E)「把男孩的數學成績跟女孩的數學成績做比較。」文章只提到男生的數學成績比女生好，是一種迷思。故 (A)、(B)、(D) 和 (E) 皆非正解。

2. 本題評量學生能否理解文意，並根據題幹說明，從文中選出一個單詞作為答案。題目詢問的是哪一個字詞意思是「使困難的情況惡化 (making a difficult situation

worse)」。第四段第六句提到「讓問題更加惡化的是 (Compounding the problem)，有些文化會把數學能力跟一個人的整體智慧連結在一起」，這使得數學焦慮加劇，故正解為 compounding。

3. 本題評量學生能否看完文章後，進行局部細節的吸收和統整，並擷取適當的文句片段作答。最後一段指出教育心理學家提出克服數學焦慮的方法及建議。給予家長和老師的建議為：try to make math less frightening「試著讓數學較不可怕」以及 avoid putting too much pressure on kids「避免給孩子太多壓力」；給予學生的建議為：try relaxation techniques「嘗試放鬆的技巧」以及 write down their worries「將擔憂寫下來」。故 (A) 正解為 avoid putting too much pressure on kids，(B) 正解為 write down their worries。

Unit 7

1. B   2. slant/Slant.
3. Facts: C; Opinions: BD

新智慧需要能分辨事實與意見

所謂「假新聞」已經受到很多關注，而且很多人都建議，你不能相信你當今所聽到或讀到的任何事。有了電腦、隨身裝置以及網路的存取，每個人都有幾乎無限量的各項資訊取得管道。在現今年代，有人會說，構成智慧的一個重要部分就是有能力辨別事實與意見。

事實是有證據支持的論述。換句話說，它們可以被檢視並且被證明屬實。事實是客觀的，意味著任何理智的人在回顧統計數字或科學研究後便能認可事實為真。

與事實不同的是，意見無法被驗證為真實或錯誤，因為它們是以個人的信念、感受或評斷為根據。然而，若有人進行研究以發掘事實來支持他或她的感受或信念，那麼意見也可以被證據證實或支持。

當談論到分辨何為事實與何為意見時，可以觀察一些關鍵字詞。例如，當人們使用像是「最好」、「比較好」和「最壞」等價值判斷字眼時，這就是一個很好的線索，代表其所說的話就是意見。「應該」這個字也是一個指標，代表你正在聆聽某人的個人觀點。當人們使用「總是」和「從未」來襯托斷然的措辭時，接下來的內容通常也是意見。

現今大部分的媒體並不完全能被稱為中立。換句話說，媒體頻道會試圖偏頗呈現他們所報導的事實，以反映特定意見或是推動特定議題。例如，一家電視臺也許會讓一個政黨看起來不錯並醜化另一個政黨，藉由報導對前者有利的故事，而給後者負面的報導。這樣的電視臺可以被視為具有「親政府」或「反政府」的觀點，視其所有人的政治傾向而定。

要銘記於心的是，真正的智慧在於能分辨事實和意見。

1. 本題評量學生能否理解文章大意，掌握文章主旨。作答線索在最後一段：real intelligence means distinguishing facts from opinions「真正的智慧在於能分辨事實和意見」。故 (B)「一個能分辨事實與看法的人，大有智慧。」為正解。
(A)「人們傾向選擇不報導假新聞的媒體頻道。」、(C)「網際網路鮮少提供準確的統計數字及科學研究。」和 (D)「本文暗示現今世代大部分的訊息都是假消息。」皆不符合文意，且過度推論。

2. 本題評量學生能否理解文意，並根據題幹說明，從文中選出一個單詞作為答案。題目詢問的是哪一個字詞意思是「提供資訊以支持某個特定看法 (to give information to support a particular opinion)」。第五段的第一和第二句指出「現今大部分的媒體並不能完全被稱為是中立的。換句話說，媒體頻道會試圖偏頗呈現 (slant) 他們所報導的事實，以反映特

定看法或是推動特定議題。」，故正解為 slant。

3. 本題評量學生能否理解文意，進行分析推論，以文章關於 facts 和 opinions 所述的特性來分類選項內容。

(A)「沒有激烈動作場景的電影總是很無聊。」、(B)「日本被認為是世上最棒的國家之一。」、(D)「美國最偉大的總統是歐巴馬。」上述三個選項使用 always、best 以及 greatest，依據第四段的敘述，含有這些字詞的敘述屬於 opinions。

(C)「化石證據顯示有些恐龍有羽毛。」、(E)「研究揭露抽菸與肺癌有關連。」、(F)「統計數字顯示，臺灣人口約兩千三百萬人左右。」上述三個選項使用 evidence、statistics 和 studies，屬於文章第二段判定為 facts 的關鍵字，均屬於 facts。

Unit 8

1. CE　2. B
3. (A) accomplishing; (B) disguise

立即可辨的探險家：丁丁

丁丁是一個由比利時藝術家艾爾吉所創造的卡通角色。他首次出現於 1940 年代一部以他名字為名的漫畫系列中，而從那時起，他就一直深受各世代漫畫迷的喜愛。讀者讚賞他英勇的行為、勇氣以及智慧，這讓他足以完成眾多危險的任務。

作為一個記者，丁丁時常揭露壞人的罪行。他的冒險經歷帶著他世界到處跑：從非洲剛果潮濕的叢林和埃及的金字塔，到亞洲喜馬拉雅山的高峰，甚至更遠。在早期系列中的一部作品〈紅海盜的寶藏〉，可看到我們的英雄乘坐著一艘鯊魚形狀的潛水艇航行在海底深部。〈月球探險〉則看到他跟他的太空人朋友登上火箭船，進入太空旅行。由於他天生就是個探險家，他也能一樣自在地駕駛飛機、直升機、船隻、火車、賽車或摩托車四處奔馳。

丁丁看起來像是個十幾歲的男孩。他瘦且不高，留著淺棕色的短髮。前面有一撮很特別的頭髮，像小波浪一樣在前額捲起。他的服裝變化很少，除非他偽裝以隱藏身分或是為特別目的而打扮。他通常穿著有領子的白色襯衫，外面套著淺藍色長袖毛衣，並將棕色褲子紮進白色襪子裡。因應天氣需求，他會穿棕色的長風衣，把領

子立起來。他忠心的白色小狗白雪總是在他身邊。丁丁和白雪,以及其他朋友,在歷險過程中一起經歷了許多事,也在很多時候拯救了彼此的性命。

儘管他外貌年輕和體態纖瘦,丁丁卻是體能強健也很敏捷。他無所畏懼,常為了要解開謎團、預防犯罪以及捕捉罪犯而將自己置於危險當中。他很聰明、善於計劃、有顆善良的心。他會願意為了幫助朋友而做任何事。

1. 本題評量學生能否掌握文章細節。(C)「丁丁很聰明而且可以保護他自己及朋友們。」作答線索在第三段最後一句及第四段最後一句;(E)「丁丁涉入一些危險的情況中,並成功阻止犯罪發生。」作答線索在第一段最後一句及第四段第二句。故 (C) 和 (E) 為正解。
(A)「丁丁歷險記是根據真實故事。」文章裡沒有提到丁丁歷險記的素材來源;(B)「丁丁出發旅行是為了尋求財富及名聲。」文章提到丁丁出發旅行的目的包含解決謎團、預防犯罪及捕捉罪犯,沒有提到是為了尋求財富及名聲;(D)「丁丁原本是個軟弱的角色,後來演變成為一個真英雄。」文章沒有說明丁丁原本角色設定為何,只提到丁丁很有勇氣並且聰明;(F)「為要追尋真正的朋友,丁丁與白雪旅行數國。」文章有提到丁丁與白雪四處冒險,且途中有其他朋友相伴,但沒有提到旅行的目的在於追尋真正的朋友。故 (A)、(B)、(D) 和 (F) 皆非正解。

2. 本題評量學生能否理解文意,掌握丁丁的外貌特性。作答線索在第三段,第二句提到丁丁留著淺棕色的短髮;第五句提到他通常穿淺藍色的套衫,裡面搭配白色有領襯衫,並著棕色長褲。根據以上描述,(B) 最符合對丁丁外型的描述,故 (B) 為正解。

3. 本題評量學生能否依據上下文脈絡,從指定的段落中各選出一個單詞,並運用語意及語法的知識,作適當的字形變化,寫出正解。
空格 (A) 的句子陳述「丁丁有足夠勇氣與智慧去阻止犯罪行為並成功**完成**各種任務。」根據文意,可以選出第一段最後一句的動詞 accomplish (完成),並依據語法 succeed in V-ing,變化成現在分詞 accomplishing,故空格 (A) 正解為 accomplishing。
空格 (B) 的句子陳述「身為**偽裝**大師,丁丁能夠到處旅行而不被任何可能認識他的人認出。」根據文意,可以選出第三段第四句的名詞 disguise (偽裝) 作為答案,故空格 (B) 正解為 disguise。

Unit 9

1. BE　2. A　3. ❹　4. D

擁有美好生活的祕訣

為了嘗試回答「何為構成美好生活的要件？」這個問題，一項來自哈佛大學的長期研究追蹤了七百二十四位研究對象，為期七十五年，從青少年期到老年。這項研究得出一個結論，和家人、朋友以及個人社群的強健社交關係可以促成更多的快樂、更好的身體健康以及更長的壽命。因此，這項研究認為人們應該努力建立並維持這類人際關係。

說到我們的人際關係，有證據顯示品質比數量更重要。換句話說，一個人有很多或是只有一些朋友並沒有那麼重要。最重要的是友誼的親密度，因此擁有一些親密的朋友可以說比擁有許多相識的人要來得更好。此研究發現，那些五十歲時對他們的人際關係感到最滿意的人，非常可能到八十歲時都還很健康。

跟我們所關心的人有良好關係似乎對我們的健康有正面的影響，然而相反的情況也成立：充滿衝突的關係會危害我們的健康。因此，我們應該做必要之事來維繫連結，並且更新或強化已經變得緊張或弱化的人際關係。我們可以藉由從事新的活動，努力讓人際關係維持生氣及意義。除了身體之外，好的人際關係會保護我們的大腦，幫助記憶更敏銳和持久。相反地，孤獨是有害的。孤立的結果造成較少的快樂、衰退的健康以及較短的壽命。

❶人們傾向於認為，累積財富和社會地位，最終可以保證美好和快樂的生活。❷然而，這項研究提供充足的證據，駁斥大眾這般的想法。❸我們可以改變我們的思考方式，做出正確決定，追求何謂真正地擁有一個美好和快樂的生活。❹因此，要擁有美好的生活，我們應該主動試著結交朋友，花更多時間與我們關心的人相處，而不是盯著電腦和手機看，變得越來越孤立。

1. 本題評量學生能否掌握文章細節。
(B)「此研究提供有關我們如何能過美好生活的概念。」和 (E)「人們可以藉由建立良好關係感到滿足並變得更健康。」皆符合文意。故 (B) 和 (E) 為正解。
(A)「人們如果有越多朋友就會越健康。」文章第二段指出，朋友多或少不重要，緊密的友誼才是最重要的；(C)「家人之間的衝突會導致更緊密的家庭情感連結。」文章第三段指出充滿衝突的關係會危害健康，並沒有提到衝突會導致更緊密的家庭情感連結；(D)「此研究證實高成就確保幸福。」文章強調確保幸福的關鍵是良好人際關係，而非高成就；(F)「當人們花比較多時間在電腦上，記憶力會更好。」文章只有於第三段提到好的人際關係幫助記憶力維持，沒有提到使用電腦與記憶力的關聯，且文末鼓勵人們花時間與人相處，而非盯著電腦。故 (A)、(C)、(D) 和 (F) 皆非正解。

2. 本題評量學生能否掌握文章大意並判斷作者的態度。作答線索在第三段，作者依據研究發現，向讀者強調維繫人際關係的必要及其好處，因此可判斷作者對該研究持認同的 (approving) 態度，故 (A) 為正解。(B) 懷疑的、(C) 幽默的、(D) 諷刺的，皆非正解。

3. 本題評量學生能否辨識哪些敘述為研究結論，哪些為作者自身想法，並加以舉證。題目詢問第四段的哪一句最能說明作者想要提供實現美好生活之依循方式的意圖。第四段的前三句為此項研究的結論及作者認同此項結論的敘述，第四句則是作者依據研究結論，提出獲得美好生活的方式：主動結交朋友，花時間與人相處，而非盯著電腦和手機看。故正解為❹。

4. 本題評量學生能否理解文章大意，進行分析推論。題目請學生依據四個人的社群媒體貼文，推測哪一位最有可能過著美好生活。Betty 的貼文為「我從朋友那拿到明天演唱會的免費門票。歡迎你跟我一起去。如果有興趣，留訊息給我。」其中有朋友送她免費樂團門票，代表好人緣，而她也歡迎朋友跟她一起去，代表她願意花時間與朋友相處，因此符合文章裡美好生活的要素，故 (D) 為正解。
Wilson：「我不知道為什麼我的朋友拒絕我的生日派對邀約。這根本不合理。」表示 Wilson 的人際關係可能不太好；Jessie：「我同學和我現在很少講話。不過，沒關係。我已

經習慣了。」表示 Jessie 缺乏人際互動；David：「天啊，那些社團活動真無趣。我一定得做這一切嗎？讓我獨自一人吧！」表示 David 不喜歡社團活動，也不想做事，只想獨處。以上皆不符研究對於擁有美好生活的結論，故皆非正解。

Unit 10

1. BF
2. PET plastic/PET (plastic) bottles/
   PET plastic./PET (plastic) bottles.
3. (A) (materials) recovery facility;
   (B) recycling

所有那些被我們丟棄的塑膠瓶，
後來怎麼了？

今天大部分的人都能認同將可回收的物質與垃圾分開是重要的。如果我們無法做到這個步驟，我們製造的大量垃圾終究會壓垮我們處理它的能力。因此，我們常在喝完東西之後，就把一次性使用的塑膠瓶放置於附近的回收桶。就保護環境而言，我們覺得我們已經盡力了。但是，接下來會發生什麼呢？

首先，垃圾桶會被清空，內容物會由卡車載至資源回收設施。這部分通常由政府的工人來做，但也可能會外包給私人公司來負責收集。在資源回收設施，材料會被分類，看看哪些可以再利用。這個決定完全是以經濟為根據。回收是一項事業，故依據規則，只有可以變賣收取利潤的物質才會被選擇。其他的會被丟棄，因為它們沒有再變賣的價值。分類的過程會以輸送帶運送材料，通過一連串的金屬探測器、磁鐵、滾輪機以及工人。

用來製作大部分瓶子的所謂「聚酯塑膠」能符合這個價值需求，所以數以千計空瓶會被扔在一起集合成堆。怪手會用巨大的爪子將它們拾起，或者由機械裝貨機用鏟子將它們鏟起來。它們被倒進機器裡，然後壓平，壓縮為重量高達一公噸的大型方塊。這些方塊會被變賣，帶到資源回收場。

接下來，這些方塊會被拆解，乾淨的塑膠會透過雷射照光穿透它們的方式被區分出來。壓扁的瓶子以肥皂清潔，並且透過加熱使標籤和瓶蓋脫落。然後機器會磨碎它們成為薄片，然後再次清洗、乾燥並且加熱。這些薄片可以轉變成布料、地毯，甚至是瓶子，延長塑膠的生命週期。

1. 本題評量學生能否掌握文章細節。
   (B)「PET 瓶子是可以回收並賺取利潤的塑膠。」作答線索在第二、三段；(F)「乾淨和綠色的塑膠被用來當作製造布料的原料。」作答線索在最後一段的最後一句。故 (B) 和 (F) 為正解。
   (A)「人類缺乏處理塑膠瓶的能力。」本文描述許多人類回收及再利用塑膠瓶的過程；(C)「所有收集起來要回收的瓶子都能被回收並再利用。」第二段指出，沒有商業利益用途的回收物質會被丟棄，不會再回收利用；(D)「在垃圾桶裡的塑膠瓶後來使用人力破壞分解。」第三段指出，塑膠瓶使用機械方式破壞分解；(E)「私人回收公司通常由政府出資挹注。」文章提到回收物的收集和運輸可能會由政府外包給私人公司，但並未提到出資挹注的描述。故 (A)、(C)、(D) 和 (E) 皆非正解。
2. 本題評量學生能否理解文意，從文中擷取題目所指涉的特定字詞作為

答案。第三段指出 PET plastic/PET (plastic) bottles 符合回收的價值，因而被集合成堆，丟到機器裡擠壓變成方塊 (cubes)，秤重後被賣給回收工廠。故正解為 PET plastic/PET (plastic) bottles。

3. 本題評量學生能否理解文意，掌握回收的步驟，並從指定的段落中選出適當字詞作為答案。第二段敘述垃圾桶被清空後，內容物會被載至 (materials) recovery facility (資源回收設施) 進行分類。有經濟價值的會被留下來成為回收物 (materials for recycling)，其餘的則因為沒有再變賣的價值 (no resale value) 而被丟棄 (be discarded)。故空格 (A) 正解為 (materials) recovery facility，空格 (B) 正解為 recycling。

Unit 11

1. a high degree of precision/
   A high degree of precision.
2. (A) repetition; (B) extreme
3. D   4. C

當機器人被設定去殺人時，會不會做得過頭了？

科技顯著地改變了這個世界。其中最驚人的發展就是機器，即機器人，它可以做許多人們以前必須自己完成的事。機械式的機器人首先於二十世紀早期開始發展，最早的電子機器人則是在 1940 年代出現。

機器人被廣泛地使用在不同產業中，以從事太無聊的工作 —— 通常是因為這些工作重複又不需要特別的技能 —— 或是太危險不適合人類工作者。舉例來說，工廠的裝配線工作需要一再重複執行相同的動作，像是組裝汽車。人類會覺得這令人厭倦，但機器人絕不會抱怨、不會生病或受傷、也不會需要休息。人類的時間需要付薪水，反之一旦購買了機器人，唯一額外的成本是定期的維修。這對公司長期來說是省錢的。

機器人也有能力可以做需要高度精確性的工作，這是超越人類的手和眼可以完成的。有些高科技的應用，如製造電腦晶片或電路板，需要如此精巧的動作控制。再者，跟人類不同的是，機器人很少犯錯。機器人可以去人類無法到達的地方，像是沒有氧氣的環境。它們可以承受可能殺死人

的極端溫度，舉例來說，像是在北極環境中的室外，或是靠近噴發火山的火山口工作。

因為這些原因，機器人逐漸被警力和軍隊使用於處理炸彈和進入罪犯及敵人躲藏的建築物。武器系統可以建置於它們身上。機器人甚至可用來殺掉威脅警察或其他平民百姓的武裝嫌犯。然而，有些人強烈反對這件事。他們宣稱這樣做太過頭，並開啟一扇通往黑暗未來的大門，其中人們得處於被機器殺死的恆常恐懼裡。如果某個程式設計師做出邪惡的選擇，而機器人執行邪惡的指令動作怎麼辦呢？或者更糟，如果機器人變成有自我意識，決定要與人類對抗的話怎麼辦呢？如果我們不謹慎小心，難以預料某天殺人機器人不會成為現實。

1. 本題評量學生能否理解文意，從文中擷取題目所指涉的特定字詞作為答案。第三段第一句提到機器人能完成需要高度精確性 (a high degree of precision) 的工作，第二句接著指出有些高科技的應用需要 such fine motor control (如此精巧的動作控制)。故正解為 a high degree of precision。

2. 本題評量學生能否依據上下文脈絡，從指定的段落中各選出一個單詞，並運用語意及語法的知識，作適當的字形變化，寫出正解。

空格 (A) 的句子陳述「機器人可以執行無需特別技巧且大量**重複**的工作，例如生產線的製造，這需要一而再地做相同的動作。」根據文意，

可以選出第二段第一句的形容詞 repetitive (重複的)，並依據語法變化成名詞 repetition (重複)，故空格 (A) 正解為 repetition。

空格 (B) 的句子陳述「從精確製造電腦晶片到在危險環境中及**極端的**溫度下工作，機器人在許多方面都超越人類的能力。」依據文意，可以選出第三段第五句的名詞 extremes (極端)，並依據語法變化成形容詞 extreme (極端的)，故空格 (B) 正解為 extreme。

3. 本題評量學生能否掌握文章大意並判斷作者的態度。作答線索在最後一段，作者提出機器人在警察武力及軍隊上的各項應用，及被設定為殺人機器的可能性。文末的 what if (要是…怎麼辦？) 質疑機器人未來往負面發展的可能性，最後一句也指出如果不謹慎小心，難以預料某天殺人機器人不會成為現實，因此可判斷作者對機器人發展持擔憂的 (worried) 態度，故 (D) 為正解。(A) 感到挫折的、(B) 樂觀的、(C) 客觀的，皆非正解。

4. 本題評量學生能否理解文意，選出哪一種機器人的應用會遭受反對。最後一段提出機器人有可能被設定為殺人機器，而此應用遭受反對。圖 (C) 符合攻擊性武器的描繪，故 (C) 為正解。

(A) 為可以完成生產線重複性工作的機器人；(B) 為可以在外太空無氧環境下工作的機器人；(D) 為可以完成製造晶片等高度精確性工作的機器人。

Unit 12

1. (A) formation; (B) compounded
2. diamonds/Diamonds.　3. BF

一閃一閃——太空中可能有鑽石嗎？

　　它們閃閃發光且著實價值不菲。它們是鑽石——由深藏在地表下的碳在承受高溫及巨大的壓力時而形成。數十億年以來，被超高溫加熱的碳逐漸因地殼重壓的重量而轉變。鑽石就是這個漫長及緩慢過程的最終產物。當然，從另一個角度來看，這只是起點。鑽石必須要用重型機械才能從地裡開採出來，並使用特別的工具及技術切割，然後再經過高度磨光後，最終才被鑲在訂婚戒指、項鍊、皇冠以及其他珠寶上。

　　科學家認為，這些好幾世紀以來一直引發人們的想像的寶石，或許也大量地存在於我們太陽系的其他星球之中。確切來說，研究人員指的是土星與木星這兩個為人熟知的巨大氣態行星。這兩個星球無一是固態的。兩者實際上皆是一團厚重的氣體，且據推測擁有固態的核心。雖然情況與我們在地球上所看到的相當不同，但是形成鑽石的要素——熱及壓力——都存在著。

　　此外，如同它們的名字所示，這些巨大氣態行星巨大無比。以這個方式來想像一下：七百六十四個地球大小的星球可以塞進土星，而一千三百二十一個這樣的星球可以塞進木星。但是沒有外層堅硬的地殼重量所產生的壓力，這些巨大氣態行星又是怎麼產生鑽石的？

　　利用他們對土星和木星所知的構成成分，科學家們創造了模型來回答這個問題。他們相信這些星球的強大重力和高溫可以將懸浮於半空中的某種化合物——甲烷——轉變成鑽石。過程是這樣發生的：當甲烷被閃電擊中，高熱就會把它轉化成微小的碳粒。當這些碳沉入這些星球的較深處，強大的壓力和高熱就可以把它轉變成鑽石。科學家以「鑽石雨」的意象來解釋這個神奇景象可能看起來的樣貌。

1. 本題評量學生能否依據上下文脈絡，從指定的段落中各選出一個單詞，並運用語意及語法的知識，作適當的字形變化，寫出正解。
　　空格 (A) 的句子陳述「當地底深處的碳遭受高溫及壓力時，鑽石的**形成**便發生。」根據文意，可以選出第一段第二句的動詞 form (形成)，並依據語法變化成名詞 formation (形成)，故空格 (A) 正解為 formation。
　　空格 (B) 的句子陳述「當甲烷跟閃電的高溫**合成**時，甲烷會轉變為碳，這是鑽石的原料。」依據文意，可以選出第四段第二句的名詞 compound (化合物)，並依據語法變化成動詞 compound (使化合) 的被動語態 compounded，故空格 (B) 正解為 compounded。

2. 本題評量學生能否理解文意，從文中擷取題目所指涉的特定字詞作為答案。第一段最後一句描述鑽石 (diamonds) 從開採到成為飾品的過

程，而第二段開頭則說科學家認為 these gems (這些寶石) 亦存在於太陽系其他行星上，因此可知第二段承接上一段，繼續討論鑽石。故正解為 diamonds。

3. 本題評量學生能否掌握文章細節。(B)「鑽石雨始於半空中，在那裡閃電將甲烷轉變為碳。」作答線索在最後一段的第二、三句；(F)「在土星和木星上，巨大的壓力和溫度可將碳轉變為鑽石。」作答線索在最後一段的第四句。故 (B) 和 (F) 為正解。
(A)「科學家一直計劃著在土星和木星開採鑽石。」文章最後一段指出，科學家建立一個模型來模擬巨大氣態行星製造鑽石的過程，並非要在土星和木星上開採鑽石。(C)「鑽石被科學家發現於土星及木星深層處。」第二段第一句提到，科學家認為「也許」(might) 在土星及木星會有鑽石存在，而最後一段第一句也提到，科學家只是建立一個模型進行探究，並未證實有鑽石存在。(D)「土星和木星因為有堅硬的外殼，所以可以製造鑽石。」第三段最後一句提到，科學家們想探究，沒有堅硬外部地殼的土星和木星，是如何製造出鑽石，並說明這兩大星球是氣態行星。由此得知這些鑽石的產生不是因為有堅硬的地殼。(E)「進行更多的研究，地球就有可能也製造出鑽石雨。」文章並未提到此項描述。故 (A)、(C)、(D) 和 (E) 皆非正解。

Unit 13

1. D 2. intake/Intake.
3. C; 4. E; 5. D

海洋汙染的受害者

海洋汙染直接衝擊到海洋生物。一些常見的受害者包含海龜、珊瑚礁、鯊魚、海鳥以及鯨魚。

海龜	海龜繁殖速度緩慢，意味著牠們的族群數目成長緩慢。因此，牠們更容易受到生態威脅的傷害。海龜會錯把塑膠袋看成食物，因塑膠的攝入而造成健康問題或死亡。
珊瑚礁	珊瑚礁是高度複雜且嬌弱的系統，由數百萬種的個別物種組合而成。牠們很容易受到環境的改變或擾動影響，像是上升的水溫、海洋酸化以及被丟入海洋的塑膠廢棄物。
鯊魚	除了環境汙染之外，鯊魚也面臨捕魚活動的威脅。被漁網或釣魚線纏住向來危及鯊魚的性命。常見的是鯊魚遊走時，牠的下頜有個魚鉤或是身上纏著釣魚線。

海鳥	像是海鷗和鵜鶘之類的海鳥，常把塑膠誤認為魚或是昆蟲。牠們把這些東西吃下肚或被纏住，這都可能導致受傷或死亡。漏油對海鳥來說也會是一場災難。油漬覆蓋牠們的羽毛，使牠們無法飛行。
鯨魚	鯨魚作為地球上最大的哺乳類動物，也受到海洋汙染的影響。上升的水溫造成鯨魚賴以為食的生物必須改變牠們的棲息地。這意味著鯨魚必須花更多時間去尋找牠們的食物來源，留給牠們較少時間進行繁殖。

1. 本題評量學生能否理解文意，尋找符合題幹「為了存活而遷徙更久更遠」(migrate longer and farther to survive) 敘述的海洋生物。作答線索在鯨魚的段落，其中第二、三句指出，因為鯨魚賴以為生的生物改變牠們的棲地，所以鯨魚必須花更多時間尋找食物來源，故 (D) 為正解。

2. 本題評量學生能否理解文意，並根據題幹說明，從文中選出一個單詞作為答案。題目詢問的是哪一個字詞意思是「攝取某物進入身體的動作 (the act of taking something into one's body)」。海龜段落的最後一句指出「海龜會錯把塑膠袋看成食物，因塑膠的攝入 (plastic intake) 而造成健康問題或死亡。」，故正解為 intake。

3–5. 本題評量學生能否整合資訊，將各個海洋生物所面臨的可能危險與選項圖案對應，並以表格方式進行統整。
珊瑚礁面臨的危險是上升的水溫、海洋酸化以及被丟入海洋的塑膠廢棄物，故空格 3 正解為 (C)；鯊魚面臨的危險是被漁網或釣魚線纏住，故空格 4 正解為 (E)；海鳥面臨的危險是誤把塑膠當作魚或昆蟲吃下肚，以及漏油，因為油漬會覆蓋羽毛而使海鳥無法飛行，故空格 5 正解為 (D)。

Unit 14

1. (A) contribute; (B) pursuit
2. collaborate/Collaborate.　3. CE

臺灣之光

「臺灣之光」這個詞首次在 2001 年的新聞報導中被提出來。這個名稱以前指的是那些在國際比賽中獲勝的臺灣人，但現在指的是那些因為他們的成就而獲得國際注目的臺灣人。這裡是兩位年輕的臺灣之光以及他們的故事。

劉安婷出生於 1989 年，是「為臺灣而教」的創辦人。安婷從她大學時代就參與弱勢團體的教育。在普林斯頓大學就讀時，她花了很多時間在不同國家工作，像是海地、柬埔寨、法國以及瑞士。最終她以優異成績拿到公共與國際事務的學士學位。然而，她不斷思考她能做些什麼來幫助她的國家。

受到她大學朋友「為美國而教」創辦人 Wendy Kopp 的啟發，安婷大學一畢業便開始跟臺灣的機構就偏鄉教育的議題合作。2014 年，安婷回到家鄉並創辦「為臺灣而教 (TFT)」，透過 TFT，她徵召在臺灣年輕的大學畢業生到偏遠的公立學校教書。

她努力貢獻於偏鄉教育，並且透過創造一個平等且高品質的教育環境來幫助資源較少的孩子。2016 年她被《富比士》雜誌獲選為亞洲三十歲以下最有影響力的三十人之一。

楊柏偉出生於 1990 年，是臺東 Sinasera 24 的主廚。二十三歲時，柏偉在一次歐洲食物雕刻錦標賽中贏得冠軍。在法國馬賽的一家米其林三星餐廳擔任廚師多年後，他決定要回到臺灣，開設一家以當地文化為特色並能體現他個性的餐廳。

柏偉的祖母是一位廚師，他母親是一位小吃攤販，所以從小他就遺傳了美食家的基因。童年時期，他常收看日本的一個美食家節目，並對每道精緻的菜餚感到驚奇。也就是那一段時間引領了柏偉去追求他的廚師夢。多年後，當柏偉在法國工作時，有一位來自臺東的民宿老闆向他聯繫，提供他擔任餐廳主廚的機會。他接受這項邀請，回到臺灣。

與其他把獲得米其林星等當作唯一且最終目標的年輕廚師不同，柏偉更執著於探索當地的食材並下功夫去實驗它們。柏偉說：「我想傳遞的是食材本身的風味，不是一堆的技巧。」

1. 本題評量學生能否依據上下文脈絡，從兩則故事中各選出一個單詞，並運用語意及語法的知識，作適當的字形變化，寫出正解。
   空格 (A) 的句子陳述「懷著她對臺灣的熱情及愛，劉安婷願意**貢獻**於教育，以幫助偏鄉的孩子。」根據文意，可以選出第一則故事第三段第一句的名詞 contribution (貢獻)，並依據語法 be willing to V，變化成動

詞 contribute (貢獻)，故空格 (A) 正解為 contribute。

空格 (B) 的句子陳述「楊柏偉回到臺東以**追求**他用當地食材為特色開一家餐廳的夢想。」根據文意，可以選出第二則故事第二段第三句的動詞 pursue (追求)，並依據語法 in pursuit of sth，變化成名詞 pursuit (追求)，故空格 (B) 正解為 pursuit。

2. 本題評量學生能否理解文意，並根據題幹說明，從指定的文中選出一個單詞作為答案。題目詢問的是哪一個字詞意思是「為達到特定目的與他人共事 (to work with someone in order to achieve a certain purpose)」。作答線索在第一則故事第二段第一句：受到同學的啟發，安婷「大學一畢業便開始跟臺灣的機構就偏鄉教育的議題合作 (collaborate)。」故正解為 collaborate。

3. 本題評量學生能否做局部細節的吸收，理解兩位臺灣之光的故事，並進行綜合分析。(C)「在他們的領域上展現卓越的成就。」兩則故事分別提到劉安婷因其教育事業獲得《富比士》雜誌的肯定，以及楊柏偉在法國米其林三星級餐廳擔任主廚，都是在各自的領域上有卓越的成就；(E)「回到家鄉實現他們的夢想。」兩則故事也提及，兩位儘管在國外接受教育或工作，但最終都回到家鄉 (臺灣) 完成他們的夢想。故 (C) 和 (E) 為正解。

(A)「在臺灣的偏鄉長大。」文中並未提到兩位在哪裡長大，只提到劉安婷關心偏鄉教育；(B)「在國外接受教育。」文中並未提到楊柏偉有在國外接受教育，只提到他在國外工作；(D)「在數個國際比賽中獲得獎項。」文中並未提到劉安婷參加國際比賽獲獎的紀錄；(F)「為臺灣犧牲自己而獲得名聲。」文中提及兩位都貢獻一己之力並完成自身夢想，而受國際肯定獲得名聲，但並未提到是因為犧牲自己，才獲得名聲。故 (A)、(B)、(D) 及 (F) 皆非正解。

錯題筆記

題號
我的選項 (錯誤原因)
答案 (正確原因)
如何運用閱讀技巧解題

題號
我的選項 (錯誤原因)
答案 (正確原因)
如何運用閱讀技巧解題

題號
我的選項 (錯誤原因)
答案 (正確原因)
如何運用閱讀技巧解題

＊可將本頁複印後使用

錯題筆記

題號
我的選項 (錯誤原因)
答案 (正確原因)
如何運用閱讀技巧解題

題號
我的選項 (錯誤原因)
答案 (正確原因)
如何運用閱讀技巧解題

題號
我的選項 (錯誤原因)
答案 (正確原因)
如何運用閱讀技巧解題

＊可將本頁複印後使用

錯題筆記

題號
我的選項 (錯誤原因)
答案 (正確原因)
如何運用閱讀技巧解題

題號
我的選項 (錯誤原因)
答案 (正確原因)
如何運用閱讀技巧解題

題號
我的選項 (錯誤原因)
答案 (正確原因)
如何運用閱讀技巧解題

＊可將本頁複印後使用

錯題筆記

題號
我的選項 (錯誤原因)
答案 (正確原因)
如何運用閱讀技巧解題

題號
我的選項 (錯誤原因)
答案 (正確原因)
如何運用閱讀技巧解題

題號
我的選項 (錯誤原因)
答案 (正確原因)
如何運用閱讀技巧解題

＊可將本頁複印後使用

錯題筆記

題號

我的選項 (錯誤原因)

答案 (正確原因)

如何運用閱讀技巧解題

題號

我的選項 (錯誤原因)

答案 (正確原因)

如何運用閱讀技巧解題

題號

我的選項 (錯誤原因)

答案 (正確原因)

如何運用閱讀技巧解題

＊可將本頁複印後使用